Microcredit Misallocation?

Microcredit Misallocation?

Social Expenditure Patterns Among Poor Borrowers

P. GARGI RAO

OXFORD
UNIVERSITY PRESS

OXFORD
UNIVERSITY PRESS

Great Clarendon Street, Oxford, OX2 6DP,
United Kingdom

Oxford University Press is a department of the University of Oxford.
It furthers the University's objective of excellence in research, scholarship,
and education by publishing worldwide. Oxford is a registered trade mark of
Oxford University Press in the UK and in certain other countries.

Published in the United States of America by Oxford University Press
546 Fifth Avenue, New York, NY 10036, United States of America.

British Library Cataloguing in Publication Data
Data available

Library of Congress Control Number: 2026935899

ISBN 9780197910580

DOI: 10.1093/9780197910573.001.0001

Printed on demand

The manufacturer's authorized representative in the EU for product safety is
Oxford University Press España S.A. of Parque Empresarial San Fernando de Henares,
Avenida de Castilla, 2 – 28830 Madrid (www.oup.es/en or product.safety@oup.com).
OUP España S.A. also acts as importer into Spain of products made by the manufacturer.

Preface

Microfinance has both economic and social impacts on poor households. These economic and social impacts affect the expenditure patterns of poor households. Poor households need financial assistance to have better economic standards of living. Therefore, microfinance has become a valuable resource not only for those in need but also for economists and anthropologists who propose strategies to combat poverty. Microfinance institutions (MFIs) have been widely regarded as an effective tool for improving the socio-economic conditions of the poor, with many studies supporting their positive impact on poverty alleviation, particularly in developing countries. However, as the poor get money through microcredit, they tend to spend it for their immediate economic and social needs to enhance their standard of living and improve their social image. Hence, there could be a plausible 'social link' through microfinance. Thus, this work investigates whether there is a link between microfinance and social expenditures.

The results of this study are based on the empirical analysis of data gathered from a randomly selected cohort of 100 borrowers who have taken a total amount of ₹10.34 lakhs in loans at an interest rate ranging between 14% and 14.60% per annum from two credit institutions: a branch of a public-sector bank and a state-run microfinance agency. The borrowers from the public-sector bank branch comprised 32 women and 18 men from a semi-urban area of Hyderabad City, whereas the borrowers from the government's microfinance facility consisted of 50 women from the rural Balapur area of Ranga Reddy District in Telangana. The study areas were randomly chosen from the list of regions and borrowers provided by the lending institutions, with no prior information about the borrowers apart from their addresses and localities as supplied by the institutions. The objective of data collection was not disclosed to the lending institutions or the borrowers to prevent bias.

The primary focus of this work is to assess how borrowers use microcredit, particularly whether they invest it in income-generating activities, as intended, or divert it to unintended purposes such as social and customary needs. MFIs provide loans with the expectation that borrowers will use them for specified economic activities to generate income, meet daily expenses, repay the loan, and reinvest the funds. The aim is to help borrowers escape poverty. However, many borrowers redirect funds towards immediate social and cultural obligations rather than using them for the intended business activities.

This work examines borrowers' expenditure behaviours and finds that they prioritize immediate obligations such as sustenance, health care, children's marriages, education, and social and religious activities over business investments. For example, the loan was often spent on sustenance (16.47%), festivals (13.78%), and children's marriages (12.77%). Other expenditures, such as health (6.72%) and food (6.05%), were lower, likely because basic services such as health care and education are free for individuals below the poverty line. However, social and traditional obligations, alongside poverty-related stigma, compel borrowers to allocate significant resources towards these needs, reducing their capacity to invest in sustainable income-generating activities.

The analysis of the 50 women borrowers who borrowed ₹479,000 from a government-managed microfinance institution reveals that only 3% (₹13,000) of their loan amount was fully used for business. An average of 5% (₹24,000) was entirely diverted to unintended purposes, 50% (₹239,000) of the loan amount was partially used for business, and 42% (₹202,000) was used for unintended needs. In total, 47% of the loan was used for unintended purposes. (Thus, the total amount spent on business was ₹239,000 + ₹13,000 = ₹252,000, and ₹24,000 + ₹202,000 = ₹226,000 was diverted.) Furthermore, 98% of the loans by the selected borrowers from this institution remained unpaid, indicating a significant failure in loan repayment.

Borrowers from the two institutions studied, which operate in different locations, shared similar behaviours in terms of loan misallocation. Both groups of borrowers consistently redirected funds intended for business purposes toward social, cultural, and customary obligations. A comparison of 100 interviewed borrowers from the 2 MFIs showed significant differences in loan utilization patterns in terms of the borrowing agency, activity, and gender. In both cases, the borrowers failed to use their loans for the intended productive activities. Instead, they prioritized immediate social obligations, which hindered their ability to invest in business ventures and generate sustainable income.

Another notable difference between the two institutions is that women borrowers from the government-managed MFI allocated only 3% of their loans fully to business, while borrowers from the bank (Institution 1) used 19.82% for the intended purpose. However, such use has not resulted in any sustainable income for the borrowers so that they can pay back the loan, utilize the money for consumption, and reinvest in the business. Additionally, 48 borrowers from both institutions secured consumption loans, and 52 refrained from taking additional loans beyond those for business activities. However, even with supplementary loans, the borrowers continued to reallocate funds to unintended uses.

Delving deep into the findings, it has come to surface that many factors influence loan diversion among small-scale borrowers. Data collected from 100 individuals involved in small enterprises and services showed that 80% of households diverted 50.72% of their funds to unintended purposes, while the remaining 20% did not divert their loans. Notably, the borrowers have not redirected their loans to any productive income-generating activities, with loan diversions primarily undertaken to meet social obligations.

This work identifies several key factors influencing loan diversion. These include the loan's purpose, the borrower's dependency ratio, supervision, and perceptions regarding repayment. These factors have significant explanatory power regarding the likelihood of loan diversion to non-productive investments. In contrast, the likelihood of not diverting the loan is influenced by factors such as the borrower's gender, the size of the borrowing group, the number of women in the group, and the borrower's perception of repayment.

Given the findings, it is essential to focus on these significant variables to ensure the effective use of limited resources and develop policies that can improve the livelihoods of small-scale borrowers. By understanding the key drivers of loan diversion, MFIs can design better strategies to ensure that loans are used for their intended purposes and help borrowers achieve long-term financial stability.

This work concludes that the diversion of loans by borrowers may be attributed to inadequate assessments of their economic, social, and sustenance needs as well as their poverty levels. Additionally, the rapid technological changes in industry and commerce create challenges for small-scale borrowers, making it difficult for them to stay competitive and invest in sustainable economic activities. Addressing these issues through better loan assessments, support, and targeted policies could help borrowers more effectively utilize microcredit and achieve financial independence.

Acknowledgements

It would not have been possible to complete this project without the initial direction given on research methodology, data collection, and literature review approach by Ms Ralitza Dimova, Professor of Development Economics, the Global Development Institute, University of Manchester, who has helped me tremendously. Without her invaluable recommendations, thoughts, and contributions, my research would have been incomplete. I thank her for her candid opinions on my data collection and research methodologies. My heartfelt thanks are also due to Dr P. Madhava Rao, my father, who, throughout my academic career, has been a constant source of wisdom and inspiration. Thank you not only for encouraging me to explore this issue but also for your support in getting it done on time. Your calm demeanour and deep knowledge have made it possible for me to succeed.

Special thanks are due to Dr. PSM Rao (Pedanana) for his timely expert guidance on the practical realities of microcredit and its effects on the economic lives of borrowers.

I would like to place on record my sincere thanks to my husband, Mr Varenya, who has been an encouragement for me to grow in my academic pursuits. His continuous prompting made it possible for me to reach this day in my academic life.

My acknowledgements would be incomplete if I did not place on record the sincere emotional support provided by my mom, G. Jyothi Rao. Mumma, you are my superhero. I do not thank you, Mom; I congratulate you on your lovely daughter's achievement.

P. Gargi Rao (She/her)

Contents

Tables

Figures

Boxes

Annexures

Abbreviations

AEMFI	Association of Ethiopian Microfinance Institutions
AIDS	acquired immunodeficiency syndrome
AIMS	Assessing the impact of microfinance
APL	above the poverty line
ARDC	Agricultural Refinance and Development Corporation
BBPSB	Bank branch of public-sector bank
BPL	below poverty line
CASH	Community Action for Self-Help
CBO	community-based organization
CEO	chief executive officer
CGAP	Consultative Group to Assist the Poor
CMG	credit management group
CSO	civil society organization
DCCB	district central cooperative bank
DECSI	Dedebit Credit and Savings Institution
DFID	Department for International Development
DHAN	Development for Human Action
DRDA	District Rural Development Agency
EMI	equated monthly instalment
FY	fiscal year
GLP	gross loan portfolio
GNPA	gross non-performing asset
GoI	Government of India
GRMFI	government-run microfinance institution
HIV	human immunodeficiency virus
ICICI	Industrial Credit and Investment Corporation of India
ID	identity card
ILO	International Labour Organization
IMO	intermediary microfinance organization
IPO	initial public offering
IRDP	Integrated Rural Development Programme
IRV	individual rural volunteer
JLG	joint-liability group
LFP	low-fee private
LLG	limited-liability loan
LWE	left-wing extremism

LIC	Life Insurance Corporation
MCS	Micro-Credit Scheme
M-CRIL	Micro-Credit Ratings International Ltd
MEPMA	Mission for Elimination of Poverty in Municipal Area
MFI	microfinance institution
MFIN	Microfinance Institutions Network
MUDRA	Micro Units Development and Refinance Agency
MYRADA	Mysore Resettlement and Development Agency
NABARD	National Bank for Agriculture and Rural Development
NBFC	non-banking financial company/non-banking financing company
NFP	not for profit
NGO	non-governmental organization
NNPA	net non-performing asset
NPA	non-performing asset
NPR	net profit ratio
NRLM	National Rural Livelihood Mission
NULM	National Urban Livelihood Mission
NUPI	Norwegian Institute of International Affairs
PACS	primary agricultural credit societies
PMJDY	Pradhan Mantri Jan Dhan Yojana
PNB	Punjab National Bank
PRADAN	Professional Assistance for Development Action
PRAYAAS	Promoting Regular and Assisted Migration for Youth and Skilled Professionals
PSB	public-sector bank
RBI	Reserve Bank of India
RCB	rural cooperative bank
RCT	randomized control trial
RFA	revolving fund assistance
RMK	Rashtriya Mahila Kosh
ROA	return on assets
ROE	return on equity
RoI	rate of interest
RRB	regional rural bank
SBLP	SHG Group–Bank Linkage Programme
SDG	Sustainable Development Goal
SERP	Society for Elimination of Rural Poverty
SEWA	Self-Employed Women's Association
SFB	small finance bank
SFMC	SIDBI Foundation for Microcredit
SGSY	Swarna Jayanti Gram Swarozgar Yojna
SHARE	SHARE Microfin Limited

SHG	Self-help group
SHI	self-help institution
SHPI	self-help group-promoting institution
SIDBI	Small Industries Development Bank of India
SJSRY	Swarna Jayanti Shahari Rojgar Yojana
SJSY	Swarna Jayanti Gram Swaraj Yojana
SLF	slum-level federation
SME	small and medium enterprise
SPMS	Social Performance Management Scheme
SRMFI	state-run microfinance institution
TAT	turn-around time
UN	United Nations
UNRISD	United Nations Research Institute for Social Development
USAID	United States Agency for International Development
VO	village-level organization
WSHG	Women's Self-Help Group
Y-O-Y	year on year

1
Introduction

1.1 The microfinance and microcredit

The loan given to the poor for income generation by the microfinance institutions or by the banks is microcredit that forms part of microfinance. All collateral-free loans to individuals belonging to low-income households (i.e. households having an annual income up to ₹300,000) are treated as microfinance loans (Reserve Bank of India, Website, 'Frequently Asked Questions'). The microfinance sector in India commemorated its Golden Jubilee in 2024, having experienced swings over the past 50 years. Established in 1974 in Gujarat with the main purpose of providing financial services to impoverished women, the Self-Employed Women's Association (SEWA) Bank was India's inaugural microfinance institution (MFI). Since then, microfinance has arguably played a significant role in financial inclusion, particularly for disadvantaged households and small enterprises in rural areas. In numerous regions of India, microcredit has served as a source of rapid money supply either for economic activities or for family expenditure.

The microfinance sector has a substantial impact, with 234 MFIs operating in the country, serving 80 million borrowers, and managing 149 million active loan accounts as of 31 March 2024. To guarantee their sustainability, MFIs must innovate their strategies, seeking opportunities for operational efficiency and resilience in difficult circumstances.

Microfinance has both economic and social impacts on poor households. These economic and social impacts have influenced the expenditure pattern of the poor households. Poor households need financial assistance to have better economic standards of living. Therefore, microfinance has become a valuable tool not only for those in need but also for economists and anthropologists who are proposing models to combat poverty. Microcredit has engendered significant optimism and

Microcredit Misallocation? P. Gargi Rao, Oxford University Press.
DOI: 10.1093/9780197910573.003.0001

expectations for accelerated poverty reduction, resulting in the 2006 Nobel Peace Prize being granted to Mohammed Yunus and the Grameen Bank for their role in diminishing global poverty.

MFIs are anticipated to assume a significant role in India's financial sector, which is still at a nascent stage. They make a significant contribution to funding businesses, accounting for most of the financial intermediation process. MFIs indirectly contributed to economic development by lending to various government agencies, households, businesses, and underserved sectors of the economy, such as rural areas, small-scale industries, and agriculture.

Many observers view these developments as a validation of microcredit as a novel approach to poverty alleviation and fostering social transformation. Financial markets are particularly susceptible to moral hazard and adverse selection issues due to the unavoidable informational asymmetries between borrowers and lenders. The former, possessing greater awareness of their unique attributes and circumstances (including their capabilities and compensations), may act in ways that conflict with the interests of the latter, generating tensions in a principal–agent relationship that must ultimately yield a mutually agreeable financial arrangement. If lenders had affordable access to borrower information and robust contract enforcement methods, they could potentially resolve the issues. Debtors who possess marketable assets could potentially pledge them to lenders as collateral.

A normal debt contract involves an individual borrower providing collateral to a lender as security for a loan, which is repaid with interest, or the collateral is forfeited if repayment fails. Regrettably, the solutions are infrequently accessible in impoverished areas, where the expense of information acquisition is substantial, the capacity for enforcement is feeble, and the possession of wealth is negligible or absent. Consequently, these groups do not constitute an appealing client base for conventional profit-maximizing financial organizations (i.e. commercial banks): the expenses are excessive, the dangers are considerable, and the loans are insufficient to render them viable clients.

Microcredit aims to address the situation by employing new procedures that compensate for want of collateral. The most renowned technique is lending to a group with combined liability (self-help groups or SHGs), rather than individual lending with restricted liability, which seeks to use local information, social capital, and peer influences present among clients in closely knit groups. The fundamental concept is that providing loans to individuals inside a group can promote collective accountability if the lending is dependent on the group's conduct. Consequently, each group member is permitted to secure an individual loan with the stipulation that all members will collectively bear the responsibility if any member defaults, regardless of the cause, whether intentional or accidental. If one member defaults and the others fail to repay the debt, all members will be subsequently denied loans. This arrangement employs peer pressure and the possibility of social consequences (e.g. disgrace and communal isolation) to encourage individuals to repay debts whenever possible. It serves as a mechanism to motivate individuals to scrutinize their group partners attentively and select their group affiliations wisely. The expenses associated with obtaining information and enforcing contracts are effectively shifted from lenders to borrowers.

The comprehensive analysis of this subject is documented in an extensive theoretical corpus concerning the microeconomics of group lending (e.g. Armendáriz de Aghion 1999; Armendáriz de Aghion and Gollier 2000; Banerjee et al. 1994; Besley and Coate 1995; Chowdhury et al. 2005; Gangopadhyay et al. 2005; Ghatak 1999, 2000; Stiglitz 1990; Varian 1990).

Although group lending remains a significant component of microcredit, there has been a gradual yet discernible shift towards more conventional, individual-based lending as microfinanciers have broadened and diversified their offerings (e.g. Armendáriz de Aghion and Morduch 2000). This work highlights only a few of the factors that may be contributing to this shift. First, it has been proposed that lending to SHGs is most effective at minimal operational scales (i.e. for small projects and loans), whereas individual lending is more advantageous for larger enterprises, even when the projects and loans remain modest and the borrowers are still relatively impoverished (e.g. Madajewicz 2003a, b). Second, enquiries have emerged regarding the dependence of group lending on peer pressure, which may induce tensions within the group, particularly among the poorest and most vulnerable members, and often appears to be overshadowed by the concerns and influences of the wider village community (e.g. Montgomery 1996). Third, concerns have been raised regarding the credibility and efficacy of peer pressure in group lending when it involves small groups of close friends or family members who possess inherent loyalties to one another (e.g. Armendáriz de Aghion and Morduch 2005). Fourth, evidence indicates that groups of strangers perform equally well, and occasionally better, than groups of close acquaintances in loan repayments, thereby challenging the significance of social ties, social capital, and social sanctions emphasized in group lending (e.g. Abbink et al. 2002; Ahlin and Townsend 2007; Sharma and Zeller 1997; Wydick 1999). Finally, certain research indicates that borrowers choose autonomy over obligations in group lending arrangements, favouring personal accountability instead (WWB 2003).

Regardless of the causes, microcredit has progressively transitioned from joint-responsibility group lending to a preference for limited-liability individual lending. The latter is evidently more appealing in certain situations, particularly when the expenses associated with peer monitoring are substantial and the social repercussions for non-compliance with group norms are minimal, as observed in areas that are more sparsely populated, heterogeneous, and anonymous. Regardless of whether it is group lending or individual lending, the primary purpose of microcredit institutions is consistent: to offer inexpensive credit to those who would otherwise be ineligible for loans, thereby alleviating poverty and inequality. Similarly, regardless of whether contracts are group-based or individual-based, several elements of microcredit arrangements remain mostly unchanged. The absence of collateral is particularly notable as it is a vital component of the anti-poverty objectives of microfinanciers. Confiscating the assets of the impoverished when they encounter repayment difficulties through no fault of their own would fundamentally contradict our mission of poverty reduction. A significant characteristic is the integration of regular, public, and collective meetings between borrowers and lenders. Such meetings can offer several advantages, even when loans are issued individually.

Regular occurrences might furnish lenders with a preliminary alert system regarding prospective issues. By incorporating public repayments, they can enhance lenders' capacity to apply pressure on prospective defaulters. By consolidating clients under a group-lending approach, the microcredit businesses can diminish the number of lenders and transaction costs. Borrowers also experience advantages, particularly from a collective perspective. Group meetings can enhance education, training, and skill development by enabling the exchange of ideas and experiences, which is especially beneficial for individuals with limited business acumen. Consequently, meetings can enhance production and mitigate default risk. Clients of microcredit banks frequently express anticipation for meetings due to the social interactions and the chance for intellectual exchange and mutual learning (WWB 2003). The funding of microcredit varies among organizations, with some depending more on subsidies while others adopt a more commercial approach.

In the latter scenario, capital is acquired through borrowing from the broader community, analogous to the operations of conventional banks. Consequently, profitability and financial self-sufficiency are critical factors, and recent years have seen an increasing focus on these aspects within the microcredit discourse. At the same time, profitability and financial self-sufficiency are not the only objectives, and their pursuit is influenced by societal considerations.

As previously stated, most of the scholarly scholarship on microcredit has been predominantly microeconomic. This work aims to provide a macroeconomic viewpoint by incorporating microcredit into a dynamic general equilibrium model of income distribution. This model delineates an overlapping-generations economy wherein agents select among three alternative occupations: subsistence production, small-scale project investment, and large-scale project investment. Subsistence activity is devoid of costs and risks, whereas project investment entails both. Agents may need to secure external funds from financial institutions to initiate a project. On a general presumption, lending occurs on an individual basis, consistent with conventional banking practices and the latest developments in microfinance. Financial market defects stem from inadequate contract enforcement, allowing borrowers to strategically default on their debts.

The microcredit model of research integrates several essential characteristics of microbusiness operations mentioned earlier, with the absence of loan collateralization, the moderation of profit motives by social considerations, and the externality effects of group meetings. These attributes are essential for rendering small-scale investment an appealing choice for agents.

In this context, it can be demonstrated that without microcredit, the population is bifurcated into individuals who can obtain substantial (collateralized) loans from conventional banks and those who cannot, relegating them to subsistence living. In these conditions, initial disparities endure, resulting in a polarized community divided between the affluent and the impoverished. This book demonstrates how the implementation of microcredit can diminish (and potentially eradicate) inequality by generating new opportunities for the impoverished through small-scale investments. By engaging in such ventures, individuals with minimal or no initial capital can improve their financial status and perhaps qualify for substantial loan access. The data indicates that the interest rate for microcredit loans exceeds that of standard bank loans. Practical observations commonly confirm this. Microloan interest rates can be exceedingly high, reaching 30–40%; although it is against the conceptual goal of a low-interest and security-free lending approach, yet the demand for microloans persists robustly.

Microcredit has provided a revolutionary alternative to conventional approaches (e.g. doles and aid programmes) designed to combat poverty and inequality. In recent years, the objectives and strategies of microcredit have intrigued scholars, advocates, and policymakers alike. This does not suggest that microcredit is a panacea; there are, indeed, instances that demonstrate the contrary. The widespread adoption of microcredit globally attests to its measured performance and sustainability.

This work aims to advance the knowledge of microcredit consequences by examining it from a hitherto overlooked social expenditure perspective.

Furthermore, a strong link between access to credit and poverty persists in economic literature. Microfinance, giving credit in small quantities to poor households, is now a tool to deal with poverty and is considered a poverty reduction strategy to target the inaccessible and provide them with loans to enable them to generate sustainable livelihoods. The character of microfinance has thus come up with a promising hand in enabling policymakers to rethink banking for the poor. There is another side to the argument, which discusses how poverty prohibits people's accessibility to the formal credit system. Therefore, a causal link between access to credit and poverty cannot go unnoticed. According to Armendariz,

> One of the notable aspects of these microfinance approaches is that improvements are possible even when lenders do not actually acquire more information. Instead, the contracts harness local information and give borrowers incentives to use their own information on their peers to the advantage of the bank. It is not that the older analyses of information problems were incorrect; it is just that they failed to consider new ideas to circumvent information problems.

The microfinance revolution started with the recognition that poor people needed access to loans and that they could use these funds productively. It has also changed the perception that poor people are not creditworthy. However, these programmes do not intend to divert the credit to unviable and avoidable extravagant expenditure, such as expenditure on social events and customary practices.

Economists have investigated the direct link between microfinance and better economic outcomes, such as improvement in health-care services, better schooling, setting up new businesses, etc. The literature highlights that there is a positive link between microfinance and these economic aspects when it comes to poor households who need money. For example, Dunford (2001) studies the integration of microfinance with the promotion of family planning/birth control and combating HIV/AIDS; Pronyk et al. (2006) found that microfinance is associated with reduced risk of physical or sexual abuse; Barnes et al. (2001) looked at the significant increase in paying the school fees for households who were treated with microfinance; Khandker (2001) found out that providing small loans to poor households led to a fall in dropout rates for children in the treatment group, etc. But there are leakages to this concept as well, and the positive link can be questioned.

As the poor get more money through microfinance, they tend to spend it on their immediate economic and social needs to enhance their standard of living and improve their social image. Therefore, microfinance may create a plausible 'social link' among its beneficiaries. Thus, this work tries to see whether there is a link between microfinance and social expenditures.

The growing concern is that households now spend more on social events and social occasions than on economic and sustenance activities. Due to social pressure from the society they live in (in the form of fear of social exclusion, stigmatization, ridicule, and peer pressure), the poor households struggle to acquire social recognition and status in society. To live up to these expectations, and due to pressure from social surroundings and circumstances, households take loans from institutions and individuals. Overall, social spending could lead to negative externalities and welfare loss, especially for poor households. Some documentation to this effect is available in the literature. Extensive literature documented a pattern of high-stakes social consumption among the poor, ranging from 'splendid funerals' (Mango et al. 2009; The Economist 2007) and 'escalating bride prices or dowries' (Dekker and Hoogeveen 2002; Rao 1993) to 'inflating social spending and lavish festivals' (Banerjee and Duflo 2007; Brown et al. 2011). Crucially, these expenditures often come at a steep cost, with ceremony-related costs frequently squeezing out essential nutritional outcomes (Chen and Zhang 2012). This phenomenon underscores the powerful societal forces that dictate the financial behaviour of low-income households. Accordingly, this study seeks to build upon these observations by investigating the specific relationship between microfinance accessibility and social expenditure patterns.

1.2 Problem statement

Microcredit, acknowledged as an efficacious policy instrument for improving the welfare of the destitute, is progressively adopted by policymakers, microfinance beneficiaries, government representatives, and donors worldwide. In this context, formal MFIs have taken on a crucial role. MFIs provide microcredit to the most destitute individuals involved in subsistence livelihoods in developing countries. (La Torre and Vento 2006). The institutions utilize creative strategies to extend microcredit to persons classified as unbankable by conventional banking systems. The novel approach includes collective financing, incremental microloans, compulsory recurring savings, consistent payback timelines, and communal collateral (Johnson and Rogaly 1997).

There is growing concern among microfinance stakeholders that microfinance organizations concentrate on business purposes over poverty alleviation aims. Until the mid-1990s, microfinance practitioners rarely prioritized sustainability as their primary goal was poverty eradication.

(Charitonenko and Rahman 2002). Since that time, microfinance organizations have systematically promoted the theme of sustainability. This indicates that MFIs in underdeveloped countries are predisposed to embrace a sustainability-first approach due to insights acquired in the microfinance sector or pressure from neoliberal donors. They have systematically assessed various measures to improve institutional sustainability. Ledgerwood (1999: 205) asserts that MFIs employ a multitude of performance indicators—namely, portfolio quality, productivity, efficiency, financial viability, profitability, leverage, capital adequacy, scale, outreach, and growth—to assess sustainability. Nevertheless, none of these indicators can ensure clients' sustainability. Social visionaries contend that the shift towards institutional sustainability has eclipsed the social objectives of MFIs (Charitonenko and Rahman 2002). They contest the abundance of 'profit' and 'commercial' focus. With this orientation, MFIs typically limit their clientele to those with strong repayment potential, target areas that are relatively inexpensive, and neglect the most impoverished individuals, which is against the conceptual goal of lending to most destitute individuals involved in subsistence livelihoods in developing countries (La Torre and Vento 2006). Additionally, MFIs would impose elevated interest rates to attain operational and financial sustainability (Charitonenko and Rahman 2002).

Conversely, certain authors and practitioners endorse a 'hybrid approach'. Consequently, MFIs are tasked with accomplishing both poverty alleviation and institutional sustainability objectives (Johnson and Rogaly 1997). Charitonenko and Rahman (2002) contend that microfinance institutions must reconcile commercial and social objectives to address mission drift. MFIs face the risk of 'social mission drift' without a defined target market and monitoring system; they are susceptible to 'commercial mission drift' unless they operate as a business and impose elevated interest rates (Charitonenko and Rahman 2002: 45).

Morduch (2000) has garnered scholarly attention by positing, 'Does the dual objective of MFIs constitute a mutually beneficial arrangement, or does it contradict the microfinance schism debate?' Theoretical conversations have unveiled divergent opinions to date. The intermediary viewpoint highlights institutional sustainability while assessing the influence of MFIs on client viability. In contrast, the beneficiary perspective underscores the importance of highlighting the benefits of microfinance for clients. Ask, Wiig (1997a) clarified that institutional sustainability cannot guarantee the viability of clients. Recently, many microfinance authors have highlighted the issue of institutional sustainability in academic journals and related publications. This work examines the loan market of MFIs from the clients' perspective. The issue at hand is the most underexplored topic. Analysing loan usage and repayment behaviours reveals consequences for client viability and the sustainability of MFIs. The work seeks to identify loan utilization behaviour, sources of repayment, reasons for delinquency or default, clients' socio-economic status, and institutional factors related to MFIs that are essential for clients' viability in the microcredit market.

The initial question pertains to the potential discrepancy between the intended purpose of loans and the actual utilization behaviour of clients within the MFI credit market (Johnson and Rogaly 1997). Empirical evidence, such as that from India, indicates that clients frequently misallocate loans for unproductive purposes (see Belay 2002; Borchgrevink et al. 2005; Getaneh 2002). Nevertheless, the data remain equivocal about the impact of loan diversion on client viability. Consequently, MFIs implement stringent measures (such as peer pressure, field personnel, and, if necessary, legal actions) to guarantee loan payback, irrespective of clients' circumstances. Impoverished clients, however, are vulnerable to unstable financial resources when repaying MFI debts. Wiig (1997b) contended that clients' reliance on insecure financial resources, such as private lenders and the liquidation of valued assets, exacerbates the cycle of poverty. Rural clients may be prone to default or delinquency due to fund misallocation, investment failure, or refusal to repay (Sanderatine 1983).

The inquiry addresses the capacity of lending institutions, which may adversely affect loan utilization and repayment behaviour. Ledgerwood (1999) contended that the design of loan products, credit delivery mechanisms, and monitoring systems of microfinance organizations should be customized to address client requirements. Clients can efficiently utilize and repay loans if MFIs successfully develop financial services. Similarly, MFIs sometimes lack skilled individuals proficient in both social development and financial management. Ledgerwood (1999) further asserted that the design of loan products, credit delivery methods, and monitoring systems of MFIs must be tailored to meet client needs.

Clients can effectively utilize and repay loans if MFIs design financial services successfully. Likewise, MFIs frequently lack qualified personnel with expertise in both social development and financial management (Ledgerwood 1999). Employee commitment, familiarity with local culture, and altruistic behaviour are critically important in the microcredit services of MFIs. Finally, the socio-economic characteristics of clients are essential. Research indicates that education, age, gender, religion, asset status, and occupation influence loan utilization and repayment practices. According to Ledgerwood (1999), effective microfinance programmes typically commence with an analysis of the attributes of target demographics.

This work aims to address the following central research questions. What are the socio-economic attributes of clients? What is the loan utilization behaviour of clients? Finally, what financial resources do clients employ to repay MFI loans?

1.3 Objectives of this work

The main objectives of the work are

a) to investigate spending on united purposes by the borrowers of microfinance,
b) to assess the extent of spending by the borrowers out of the loan taken and the percentage of borrowers resorting to diverting the loan towards unintended purposes,
c) to provide policy recommendations on addressing the issues of diversion and developing new ways for income generation.

1.4 Others' findings in the area

The MFIs are often seen by the aid practitioners as a transparently effective means of improving the position of the poor. There is an abundance of literature on microfinance available today. A vast majority of the literature reads like an evaluation study and impact on income generation. No literature is seen to be clearly focusing on the extent of leakages in microcredit obtained for economic activities, credit being diverted towards non-productive, domestic purposes, social events, and other obligations. The literature reviewed reveals many impact evaluation studies that look at the success of MFIs in helping and aiding the poor for better economic outcomes. Studies from Africa and Asia-Pacific countries reveal that microfinance has been utilized more for social expenditures. Also, little is known about the effectiveness of targeting the 'core poor'—which is a major flaw in the interventions identified by the MFIs. However, keeping in mind the wider area of microfinance knowledge, this work focuses on some earlier studies relevant to it. Moreover, it is the general perception and belief that social responsibilities, cultural rituals, traditions, customs, festivals, and other day-to-day non-commercial needs play a dominant role in the lives of many who are in financial distress. These events even decide the quantum of credit requirements and expenditure patterns of borrowers from MFIs.

1.5 The questions before us

Many questions emerge as we delve deeper into the concept and practice of microfinance in India. This work tries to bring together the empirical analysis of the impact of microfinance on household expenditure of the poor in Telangana state in India using the primary and secondary data from the field. The work tries to analyse three main questions:

a) Does household expenditure depend on social traditions?
b) Does microfinance lead to more expenditure on social occasions because money is readily available? Or are there social compulsions to spend money on social events by borrowing from any sources?
c) Can we develop a policy framework covering both the social spending and income generation among the poor?

This work focuses on the intent of microfinance conceptually and how it has drifted from its original intent of income generation for the borrowers to enable them to sustain their living. The conceptually very strong and practically very weak approach of microcredit is to be examined not based on emotions and observations but rather on practical data collected from the field and establishing the harsh realities. This work does exactly the same. The approach uses the readily available research on the successes of microfinance. Thus, it constitutes a re-examination of data derived from secondary data sets generated by various MFIs, specifically focusing on the National Bank for Agriculture and Rural Development's (NABARD's) status of MFIs, data sets produced by the state-run MFI (SRMFI) in Telangana state of India, and the primary data gathered by the author. The selection of a research field reveals the existence of numerous MFIs operating in the Telugu states, particularly in Telangana. Following the microfinance crisis in Andhra Pradesh (see Annexure V), it may be noted that there are self-imposed restrictions by MFIs on their lending activities and constraints imposed by state governments and the Central Bank. Consequently, a mere 11 public-sector banks, 7 private-sector banks, 10 district cooperative central banks, 2 regional rural banks, and 5 private-sector non-banking financial institutions are providing loans for micro activities. Most importantly, the study uses the data collected from household surveys of various households living in the slums of Hyderabad.

1.6 Approach

The problem statement describes the diversion of loans by the poor for unintended purposes of the loan. Although poverty reduction is the main intention of microcredit, the poorer borrowers have more social commitments than investing the loan money into income-generation activities while taking care of their family's consumption and meeting the social, religious, and cultural commitments. Randomized control trials, identification of dependent and independent variables, finding regressions, and analysing the data using statistical and econometric tools are not possible where the spending behaviour of the poor is based more on their customs, beliefs, practices, sentiments, and immediate needs than on business and investment needs. The main purpose is to establish with evidence that the intended purpose of the microcredit is not served. Accordingly, the author uses graphs, percentages, and tables to present the findings. This is more elaborately discussed in Chapter 4. The research investigates the loans obtained and used by borrowers in small amounts from two institutions: the rural branch of a public-sector bank and the SRMFI in Telangana.

Furthermore, this work examines the trajectory of microfinance in Telangana, part of undivided Andhra Pradesh, India, where proponents regard it as having achieved significant success. In India, two predominant microfinance models exist: one is government-led, while the other is driven by private organizations, many of which are based in undivided Andhra Pradesh. The client and loan numbers in Accounts Payable surpassed the national average. Nonetheless, this did not avert the industry from nearing a crisis in 2006, with microfinance organizations facing allegations of employing predatory practices that resulted in client suicides, ultimately culminating in a complete standstill as stakeholder interests conflicted in 2010. On the one hand, it effectively halted the operations of organizations, thereby restricting the access of the impoverished in Telugu states to microfinance; on the other hand, it ostensibly offered respite to clients who were being subjected to harassment by MFIs and possessed minimal power to counteract this.

The available literature suggests that microfinance positively impacts social expenditure. The indicative results suggest that there may be a positive effect on festival and wedding spending when considered as a percentage of health and education expenditures. To investigate the microcredit utility conceptually and in practice, this book is divided into six focused chapters.

- Chapter 1 (this chapter) deals with the introduction to the work, which traces the evidence of formulating the questions for examination and investigation.
- Chapter 2 explains the trends in microfinance and traces the history of microfinance in India. It explains how it evolved and institutionalized over time and the current trends and approaches in microfinance.
- Chapter 3 looks at what others have said about microfinance by succinctly reviewing their works. This chapter looks at the evidence from past work on social spending, health, and education.
- Chapter 4 explains the investigation and approach methodology applied to this work. This chapter also explains why conventional econometric models are not used in analysing the data.

- Chapter 5 is dedicated to explaining the findings, results analysis, and results of the study.
- Chapter 6 focuses on conclusions and recommendations.

The observations and available data analysis are conveyed with the help of graphs, tables, charts, and figures throughout.

2

Microfinance in India

Major Trends

2.1 Introduction

Chapter 1 introduced microfinance, the purpose and objectives of this book, and the layout of the work. This chapter examines the major trends in microfinance or microcredit and how they evolved over the years. Between 2000 and 2010, Indian microfinance institutions underwent significant fluctuations. In 2012, the Reserve Bank of India (RBI) intervened to avert the collapse of the microlending sector following the Andhra Pradesh crisis. In response to the Y. H. Malegam panel recommendations, the RBI established the non-banking financial company–microfinance institution (NBFC–MFI) category, subjecting larger NBFC–MFIs to Central Bank oversight to ensure operational regulation. The 2010 MFI crisis was fundamentally the result of imprudent lending practices. The state government of former Andhra Pradesh implemented a stringent law to curtail MFI operations due to unethical lending and recovery practices by certain companies.

2.2 Major trends

Before delving into the trends in microfinance, specifically the microcredit part of this work, let us look at the current level of microcredit operating in the market in India. As of 30 June 2024, NBFC–MFIs are the predominant providers of microcredit, with an outstanding loan amount of ₹168,747 crore, with 234 MFIs operating in the country, serving 80 million borrowers, and managing 149 million active loan accounts representing 39.8% of the total industry portfolio. Banks possess

Microcredit Misallocation? P. Gargi Rao, Oxford University Press. © P. Gargi Rao 2026.
DOI: 10.1093/9780197910573.003.0002

the second largest portion of the microcredit portfolio, with total outstanding loans amounting to ₹138,003 crore, constituting 32.5% of the overall microcredit sector.

Small finance banks (SFBs) possess an outstanding loan amount of ₹72,430 crore, accounting for a total share of 17.%. NBFCs comprise 9.7%, while other MFIs represent 1.0% of the total sector. Table 2.1 presents the essential portfolio and outreach metrics of the five primary categories of microfinance lenders.

In addition to MFIs, the National Rural Livelihood Mission (NRLM) plays a crucial role in the microfinance sector via its Self-Help Group–Bank Linkage Programme (SBLP). As of June 2024, approximately 88.4 lakh self-help groups (SHGs) possessed an outstanding portfolio of ₹2,58,624 crore, averaging ₹2,92,700 per SHG. As of 30 June 2024, the total size of the universe regarding gross loan portfolio (GLP) is ₹ 6,83,069 crore in relation to SHG outreach.

Historically, microfinance, which originated as microcredit, began informally in India when rural money lenders provided small loans secured by pledges of land, houses, cattle, gold ornaments, and (in some extreme cases) the sons and daughters of the borrowers. In 1954, the All-India Rural Credit Survey report revealed that informal lending—overwhelmingly by private moneylenders—dominated the rural credit space with a 70% share, whereas cooperatives and commercial banks provided only 6.4% and 0.9% of credit, respectively.

The purposes for which money was borrowed from the money lenders varied (See Box 2.1). It covered farming activities, health, marriage, and

Table 2.1 Status of microcredit (30 June 2024)

Types of Entity	No of Entities	Unique Borrowers (Cr)	Active Loan Accounts (Cr)	Portfolio Outstanding (Cr)
NBFC – MFIs	86	3.4	6.0	1,68,747 (39.75%)
Banks	13	2.4	5.1	1,38,003 (32.51%)
SFB	10	2.0	2.4	72,430 (17.06%)
NBFC	83	0.1	1.3	41,076 (9.68%)
Others	36	0.1	0.1	4,189 (1.00%)
Totals	228	8.0	14.9	4,24,445 (100%)

Source: mfinindia.org.

Box 2.1 Key microfinance highlights

- About 99% of microfinance loans in India are provided to women from low-income households.
- Around 98% of loans are provided through the JLG lending model, in which a group of between five and ten customers collectively applies for loans and agrees to support each other in repaying the loans if any member of the group encounters difficulties with repayment. This group model brings efficiencies in operational expenses and leverages social collateral towards underwriting and against the risks of defaults.
- Microfinance loans are collateral-free. Outflows on account of repayment of monthly loan obligations shall be subject to a limit of a maximum of 50% of the monthly household income.
- The microfinance industry has a diverse supply side with multiple lenders (nearly 194), including banks, SFBs, NBFC–MFIs and NBFCs.
- The industry has an outreach in almost 632 districts of India. In terms of geographic spread, 76% of the loan portfolio is rural and 24% is urban.
- Loans are primarily for income-generating activities but are also taken for household expenses such as education, health, and housing.
- Except for non-profit MFIs, the RBI regulates all lenders.

Source: Compiled by the author.

other customs and practices in rural areas. Borrowing money for small business activities was there, but evidence is lacking as to its extent. One of the old blockbuster movies of the first decade of post-independence India, *Mother India* (a Hindi movie of 1957), mostly depicts the rural indebtedness. Individual borrowers, who had assets to forfeit in the event of non-repayment of loans with interest, were the only ones eligible for this lending activity. Sometimes, the interest itself overshot the principal amount. Group financing was not known in those days.

When it comes to addressing the inherent flaws in the rural credit market that had previously prevented formal credit agencies from providing financial services to the poor, the group-based credit delivery mechanism has received noticeably more attention from financial service providers. The performance of these programmes has been credited to the groundbreaking group-based financial provisioning model developed by Grameen in Bangladesh, which prefers to lend to groups of co-signers rather than individual borrowers. The group-lending mechanisms and the shift in attitudes regarding banking were, in fact, crucial to the model's success. The policymakers and development planners in the countries of Asia, Africa, and Latin America were influenced by Grameen's new approach to group lending, which promises high repayment rates from the poor borrower without any loan subsidies. However, further advances led to a variety of group-based microfinance schemes that are now in use in many nations and contextualized for the specific environments there.

The major banks did not even begin extending branch networks into rural areas until 1954. Since then, there have been substantial efforts to expand the network of cooperative banks. When 14 major banks were nationalized in 1969, there was a significant push to expand the branch network in rural areas and increase direct lending to small businesses and farmers by establishing priority sector lending. Major moves in this direction included the establishment of regional rural banks in 1975, the National Bank for Agriculture and Rural Development (NABARD) in 1982, and most importantly, the initiation of the Integrated Rural Development Programme (IRDP) in 1982. The credit schemes included both an outright capital subsidy and discounted interest rates. Nevertheless, all of these initiatives, with the intended goal of providing affordable loans to the underprivileged, were in vain. These programmes failed because of poor management and bureaucratic control over the cash (Table 2.2).

Above all, because they were unable to secure collateral, women workers in the unorganized sector were mostly left 'untouched'. Thereby, until NABARD's efforts through its pilot project in Karnataka (1991–92) to link SHGs with formal banks, mediated through the non-governmental organization (NGO) Mysore Resettlement and Development Agency (MYRADA), which achieved good results, women workers could not

Table 2.2 Types of microcredit provider in India

Categories of provider	Legal framework governing their activities
a) Domestic commercial banks, public-sector banks, private-sector banks, local area banks	(i) RBI Act 1934 (ii) BR Act 1949 (iii) SBI Act (iv) SBI Subsidiaries Act (v) Acquisition and Transfer of Undertakings Act 1970 and 1980
b) Regional rural banks	(i) RRB Act 1976 (ii) RBI Act 1934 (iii) BK Act 1949
c) Cooperative banks	(i) Co-operative Societies Act (ii) BR Act 1949 (AACS) (iii) RBI Act 1934 (for scheduled banks)
d) Cooperative societies	(i) State legislation such as MACS
e) Registered NBFCs	(i) RBI Act 1934 (ii) Companies Act 1956
f) Unregistered NBFCs (Non-banking finance company-led microfinance institutions (NBFC–MFIs))	(i) NBFCS carrying on the business of an FI prior to the coming into force of the RBI Amendment Act 2007, whose request for renewal of certificate is yet to be accepted by the RBI
h) Other providers such as societies, trusts, etc.	(i) Societies Registration Act '60 (ii) Indian Trusts Act (iii) Chapter IIIC of RBI Acts '34 (iv) State Money Lenders Act
Eligibility for microcredit	Borrowers' annual income from all sources should not exceed ₹125,000 per annum or ₹300,000 per annum as per RBI FAQs, 2022
Loan amount	Not to exceed ₹300,000; minimum loan: ₹5,000

Source: Created by the author using data collected from various Reserve Bank of India (RBI), National Bank for Agriculture and Rural Development (NABARD), and Regional Rural Banks (RRB) documents.

easily obtain the official loans. MYRADA was institutionalized in 1996 by the RBI as a regular lending activity of banks under the priority sector and service area approach because of its evident success in bridging the gap between banks and the poor.

The goal of NABARD's plan was to address the credit demand–supply imbalance for women workers. The conventional financial institutions of the nation had not adequately addressed the credit needs of the poor, notably women and those in the unorganized sector. Diverse experiences in this industry had led to the requirement for a quasi-formal credit distribution mechanism that was client-friendly, had straightforward and minimal procedures, was quick to disburse money, and had flexible repayment terms. Additionally, the plan was for the credit system to link savings and thrift with credit while maintaining relatively low transaction costs for both lenders and borrowers. The 'Rashtriya Mahila Kosh' ('National Credit Fund for Women') was founded by the Indian government in 1993 with these goals in mind (RMK 2000).

Although the government attempted to launch the SHG movement with the MYRADA experiment in the early 1990s, the formation of the Self-Employed Women's Association (SEWA) Bank had already set the stage for the microfinance movement in India. The SEWA members founded SEWA Bank, a pioneering institution in India's microfinance industry that exclusively serves the requirements of female employees.

One of the first organizations to recognize the need for affordable financing for underprivileged workers to stock up on the tools and working capital for their profession was the SEWA of Gujarat, led by Ela R. Bhatt (Banerjee 1999). The group established the SEWA Mahila Sahakari Bank in 1974 with 4,000 depositors because traditional financial institutions declined to make the effort. The SEWA Bank's objectives are the same as those of microcredit programmes; it has also worked to support small-scale regular savings by women without assets and to provide them with credit, particularly for their income-generating activities. The bank encourages SEWA members to attempt to increase the productivity of their work even though they initially only have one job. In order to help women better plan for the future, the bank offers them financial counselling, assists them with market and feasibility assessments, offers them technical training, and creates a specific programme called 'financial planning' (SEWA 1999).

As a result of globalization processes and the subsequent banking reforms in India in the early 1990s, commercial banks in particular, and organizations that provide institutional credit in general, gradually left rural areas. Formal financial intermediaries, non-governmental groups, development practitioners, and politicians in India were motivated to test the model by the successes from Latin America and Africa and the popularity of group-based credit innovations in Bangladesh. NABARD launched the SHG–Bank Linkage Initiative in 1992, which significantly accelerated the microfinance movement in India. To support SHGs, provide wholesale loans to NGOs and non-bank institutions for on-lending to the poor, and encourage micro-entrepreneurship through training, a significant number of national and international donor organizations came together in the end. There have been an enormous number of them since the SHG movement began; by 2004–05, there were more than 16.2 lakh; as of 31 March 2022, there were over 11 million SHGs as per NABARD; and as of early 2025, India had approximately 9.1–10.5 million SHGs, with around 90.90 lakh (9.09 million) reported in February 2025 by the Ministry of Rural Development. It should be emphasized that, despite variations in their operating strategies, all supporters of SHGs share a commitment to eradicating poverty by giving financial services to the less fortunate.

The Government of India (GoI) launched a nationwide promotion of the microfinance programme known as Swarna Jayanti Gram Swarozgar Yojna (SGSY) in 1999 in response to the need to identify and focus on the beneficiaries under the group-based loan programmes. The SGSY is designed as a comprehensive programme of microenterprise development that targets individuals living below the poverty line (BPL) and focuses on forming SHGs, providing them with financing, and other support services that also include a significant amount of subsidy. Notably, by February 2025, the SGSY initiative had resulted in the formation of more than 90 lakh SHGs.

Lending to SHGs is to be viewed as normal business activity of the banks, and the RBI recognized the group-based credit delivery system as an innovative technique rather than a targeted credit programme (RBI 1996). When giving bank loans to the groups, the SBLP, which is promoted by NABARD, adheres to the guidelines of the RBI's credit policy. It rejects the idea of giving the member borrower any kind of subsidy. Additionally, it is not targeted. However, encouraging women borrowers from the poorer classes to join the SHG is generally the focus. SGSY places a strong focus on subsidy-led targeted group-promotional microfinance programmes. Despite the competing interests of financial intermediaries and the government, the two SHG programmes are present across the country. This has made researchers curious about the issues that influenced the programmes' design, their reach across regions and population groups, and their pattern of growth over time. Although these issues fall under the purview of this book, the current chapter, concentrating on Indian microfinance programmes, analyses the various strategies used by institutions that promote microfinance and the trends and patterns of the programmes and explores the connection between programme outreach and poverty across Indian states. Thus, the institutional support of apex financial agencies, as well as national and foreign donor organizations, is covered in section 2.3. This support is essential for the growth of microfinance in India.

2.3 Institutional support and macrofinancial policy

Although the vehicles for loan extension have been evolving steadily over time (Capoor 2001), microcredit has been a focus area for the RBI. Notably, in 1992, the connection between SHGs and banks first began as part of NABARD's pilot project. According to the instructions of the pilot project, the banks' lending decisions to SHGs would be generally guided by norms relating to margin and security as well as scales of funding and unit cost. If banks thought it essential, they might deviate from the rules. These exceptions to the margin and security requirements, however, only applied to the SHGs that would receive funding through the pilot project. The pilot project's resounding success prompted the development of a regulatory and policy framework that supports the promotion of SHGs. In 1994, the RBI established a high-level working group to recommend such actions.

In 1996, banks were encouraged to implement a variety of initiatives to strengthen the SBLP in accordance with the working group's recommendations. According to the proposals made, eliminating SHGs was to be regarded as regular bank business and acknowledged as a credit innovation rather than a targeted credit programme. The banks were entirely responsible for formulating their own models and selecting any conduit or intermediary for microcredit distribution. They were also permitted to establish their own lending standards while taking local conditions into consideration. The goal is to offer the highest amount of freedom possible when it comes to microloans, while also considering the local environment and the necessity to help the poor obtain financing. Additionally, according to the standards, microcredit should be a crucial component of the bank's business credit plan and should undergo a quarterly assessment at the highest level. The bank must keep records of and submit reports on 'advances to SHGs and/or NGOs for on-lending to SHGs', with the requirement that these loans be counted towards 'weaker-section'" credit. The working group acknowledges that increasing the flow of microcredit requires a simple system with minimal requirements for procedures and documentation. The loan application forms, processes, and NABARD's circular letter no. NB.DPD.FS.4631/92-A/91-92, dated 26 February 1992, provided banks with comprehensive operational directions for carrying out the initiative. Simple paperwork would make it easier to provide quick and hassle-free microcredit. Since the inability to mobilize savings is a significant barrier to providing microfinance, significant relaxations have been made to the rules governing registration, asset maintenance, and reserve fund requirements for non-profit NBFCs and MFIs. The registration and prudential requirements for MFIs registered as not-for-profit NBFCs have been waived. The interest rates that apply to loans issued by banks to microcredit organizations or by microcredit organizations to the SHGs/member beneficiaries have, crucially, been completely left up to their discretion as part of the country's comprehensive financial sector reforms.

Additionally, the Task Force on Supportive Policy and Regulatory Framework for Microfinance, established by NABARD, offered more beneficial proposals for fostering the sector's rapid expansion in 1999–2000. However, the RBI looked at several concerns relating to the distribution of microloans, and in the mid-term review of the monetary and credit policy for 2003–04, banks were recommended to give their branches sufficient incentives to finance SHGs. The review also underlines the need for a completely hassle-free method of microfinancing SHGs, which may also cover consumption costs.

The SHG programme was officially extended to regional rural banks (RRBs) in 1992 as a pilot project, although RRBs were encouraged to become involved as promoting institutions later on. The programme was formally mainstreamed with banks (including RRBs) in 1995, and with cooperative banks as well to facilitate easier and more meaningful banking with the poor. A total of 545 institutions, including 47 commercial banks, 158 RRBs, and 340 cooperatives, were taking part in the linking programme as of 31 March 2006 (NABARD 2006). The commercial banks, out of the three types of banks mentioned above, have played the most significant part in the development of SHGs. According to the most recent annual policy statement of the RBI, the country's main microfinance initiative is still the programme that links SHGs with the banking sector. As many as 1,996,488 (provisional) SHGs were connected to banks by the end of March 2006, and a total of ₹9,495 crore had been lent to SHGs. The yearly target of credit linkage to 385,000 SHGs for the year has been increased according to the Union Budget 2006–07. On 25 January 2006, banks were given permission to use the services of NGOs/SHGs, MFIs, and other civil society organizations (CSOs) as intermediaries in providing financial and banking services using the business facilitator and correspondent models, based on the recommendations of the Khan Committee.

The GoI has acknowledged the significance and applicability of the SBLP in India's rural development as an innovative strategy for reaching and empowering the underserved and unreached poor, and the GoI has now designated the initiative as a national priority. To promote foreign involvement in microfinance enterprises, the GoI has permitted foreign direct investment in micro/rural lending. The government advocates for a change from a minimalist approach, which only provides financial intermediation, to an integrated approach, which includes credit provisions along with other support services, including the provision of enterprise development services. The government sees group-based credit innovation as a major strategy for reducing poverty. The formation of the Microfinance Development Fund is a significant development in this area. This fund was established by NABARD to broadly support the following activities: (i) providing training and exposure to SHG members, partner NGOs, banks, and government agencies; (ii) providing start-up funds to MFIs and covering their initial operational deficits; (iii) covering the costs associated with the formation and upkeep of SHGs; (iv) developing new delivery mechanisms; and (v) promoting research, action research, management information systems, and the dissemination of best practices. Thus, it is anticipated that this fund will address institutional and delivery challenges such as institutional growth and transformation, governance, access to new funding sources, institutional capacity building, and scaling up. Additionally, group-based credit programmes were adopted as a key technique by the Ministries of Rural Development and Women and Child Development to combat poverty. Section 2.4 provides coverage of these programmes. Additionally, NABARD and the Small Industries Development Bank of India (SIDBI) are two apex-level financial institutions that support, promote, and finance microfinance programmes in the nation. Several international organizations, including the World Bank, the United States Agency for International Development (USAID), the United Nations, and the Department for International Development (DFID), in addition to Indian financial intermediaries, are actively promoting group-based credit innovation for the diversification of rural livelihood methods to eradicate poverty.

2.3.1 Swarnajayanti Gram Swarozgar Yojana (SGSY)

Since April 1999, the Ministry of Rural Development, GoI, has made the SGSY programme active as a key method to reduce poverty. Beneficiaries of SGSY are referred to as Swarozgaris. Both individuals and organizations can be Swarozgaris. However, SGSY places a strong focus on the group approach, in which the rural poor are grouped into SHGs in accordance with the widely adopted NABARD model. In either event, identifying families for assistance under SGSY will use the list of BPL households identified during the BPL census, officially approved by the Gram Sabha. SHG members must be chosen from the Gram Sabha-approved BPL list. The fundamental goal of SGSY is to raise the Swarozgaris, or helped poor households, beyond the poverty line by assuring an appreciable sustained level of income over time (GoI 1999). This goal will be accomplished, among other things, by organizing the rural poor into SHGs through a process of social mobilization, their capacity building and training, and the distribution of assets that can generate income.

2.4 The target group of SGSY

SHGs, as the name itself suggests, are not official groups, despite being supported by local government agencies. The establishment, growth, and strengthening of the groups so that they can become self-managed people's organizations at the grassroots level is the promoter's role. The promoter exploits the existing ties within caste, community, family, place of origin, activity, etc. to form affinity groups and encourage people to band together. An SHG may have between 10 and 20 members. Every member of the group should come from a low-income family. Nonetheless, if agreed by the BPL members of the SHG, a maximum of 30% of the members may come from the families above the poverty line living in the nearby areas. SGSY is a centrally sponsored rural self-employment programme, and the costs of the programme will be split 75:25 between the centre and the states. The central allocation for the states shall be distributed based on the prevalence of poverty within them. They may register under the GoI's society registration legislation and may also be federated. Nonetheless, this figure may vary from 5 to 20 in arduous environments such as deserts, hills, and areas with scattered and sparse inhabitants, as well as in instances with minimal irrigation and those with disabilities. The State Level SGSY Committee is tasked with identifying problematic areas, and membership relaxation will be permitted solely in certain locations. This chapter discusses families in occupational groups such as agricultural workers, marginal farmers, and craftspeople who are slightly above the poverty line or those excluded from the BPL list but permitted to join the SHG. It is important to note that SGSY is a national government project. It appropriately prioritizes the needs of vulnerable populations, including women and individuals with disabilities. Furthermore, an objective is established whereby 50% of the total groups formed in each block must be exclusively for women to advance women's SHGs.

2.5 Financial intermediaries in SGSY

The provision of a revolving fund is a distinct element of SGSY capacity enhancement. SHGs are eligible to obtain the revolving fund of ₹25,000 from the bank as a cash credit facility once they have been in operation for around six months and have shown ability as a viable group. It includes a ₹1,000,000 subsidy that is adjusted to the bank by the District Rural Development Agency (DRDA). The SHGs become eligible to receive assistance for economic activities after successfully repaying the revolving fund assistance and redeeming the loan, which is calculated by subtracting the subsidy value of ₹1,000. Loans and subsidies are two methods employed to achieve this. An SHG may get this support through one of two methods: first, by offering a loan or an SGSY to its members, contingent upon the potential Swarozgaris' ability and willingness to participate in income-generating activities within certain sectors. Second, an SHG may extend a loan combined with a subsidy to the organization if all members opt to participate in a collective activity. Ideally, the group should engage in a singular activity under the group loan; nevertheless, if necessary, the group may carry out multiple activities. In both instances, the group will serve as collateral for the bank to ensure prompt loan repayment. The loan will be sanctioned in the name of the group.

2.6 Organizational support for SGSY

A facilitator collaborating intimately with local communities may be crucial for the establishment and development of the organization. Consequently, SGSY programmes first incorporated the notion of offering support services to SHGs, with the stipulation that subsidies would not be accessible to above-the-poverty-line (APL) members. They are also eligible to serve as office holders of SHGs. The DRDA functions as the principal implementing agency for SGSY at the district level. The personnel are the DRDA, NGOs, community-based organizations (CBOs), and the network of community coordinators. A community coordinator could be assigned the task of overseeing 10–15 SHGs in a geographic cluster made up of 4–5 communities within a range of 4–5 kilometres. The DRDA may plan training and exposure events for the group facilitators, and these facilitators should communicate with the DRDA frequently to gather feedback on their respective groups.

The SGSY subsidy would be standardized at 30% of the project cost with a minimum of ₹7,500. However, for Scheduled Castes (SC) and Scheduled Tribes (ST), these will be either 50% or ₹100,000, whichever is greater. The subsidy would be at 50% of the project cost for Swarozgari groups (SHGs), limited to a per capita subsidy of ₹1000 or ₹1.25 lakh, whichever is less. Other advantages include talent development, marketing assistance, livestock insurance, and group life insurance. However, the official rules are far more exaggerated when compared to what is actually practiced in the field.

2.7 National Bank for Agricultural and Rural Development (NABARD)

NABARD came into existence on 12 July 1982 by transferring the agricultural credit functions of the RBI and the refinance functions of the then Agricultural Refinance and Development Corporation (ARDC). It was dedicated to the service of the nation by the late Prime Minister Smt Indira Gandhi on 5 November 1982. This was almost seven years after RRBs were established in 1975 through an ordinance to extend microcredit benefits for agriculture, allied agriculture activities, rural artisans, small businesses, and rural professionals who had hitherto been deprived of institutional credit. In 1987, NABARD approved a grant of ₹10 lakh from its research and development budget to MYRADA as seed money to the credit management groups (CMGs) that it was promoting (Jayaraman 2001). This was the beginning of NABARD's microfinance promotion. The goal of the grant programme was to make it easier to accumulate a thrift fund and to provide CMG members with margin funds so that they could access the formal credit system. Due to the experiment's success, an experimental project linking 500 SHGs with banks was commissioned in 1992 (NABARD 1995). This project, known as the SHG–bank linkage, was anticipated to benefit the banking industry from the perspectives of both increasing operational efficiency and fulfilling its social aim of reaching the targeted. Importantly, NABARD encouraged NGOs to act as financial intermediaries for banks or other formal financial institutions to support group-based credit innovation. The fundamental tenet of the scheme was that, with effect from 1 January 1988, a group life insurance programme was created for Swarozgaris (self-employed) who were at least 18 years old but not yet 60 years old. This programme is in effect from the date the asset is given to the Swarozgari until the Swarozgari reaches the age of 60 or for a period of five years after the coverage, whichever comes first. In the event of a natural death, ₹5,000 will be payable by the Life Insurance Corporation (LIC) to the deceased's nominee. In the event of an accident-related death, the LIC will be required to make a payment of ₹1,000. The NGO MYRADA operates in the nation's southern part. NABARD's linkage models aim to create a synergy between banks with the financial wherewithal and NGOs with the capacity to organize the underprivileged and increase their potential to access bank loans.

In contrast to the well-known Grameen Bank in many developing nations, the NABARD model of group-based credit innovation in India is unique (Harper 2005). Although there are similarities between SHGs and Grameen in terms of regular meeting dates, mobilizing savings, and peer selection during group creation, the most significant difference is joint liability, which Grameen practices. The importance of this component in reducing the information asymmetries and moral hazard that previously limited the ability of formal lenders to participate in the rural credit market has been highlighted in numerous pieces of theoretical research on credit market modelling (Carter 1995; Stiglitz and Weiss 1981). However, the concept of 'joint liability' was criticized for its shallow scope of application and detrimental impacts on the extremely underprivileged or the most vulnerable (Dichter 1996; Morduch 2000). Likewise, the SHG model focused on 'voluntary collective action' by the members to improve the institution's efficiency and sustainability.

2.8 A different target group for NABARD

NABARD has basically targeted SHGs to encourage microfinance. SHGs promoted by NABARD do not have any eligibility requirements, in contrast to SGSY. The participants choose among themselves to form a group in a nearby location, such as the same hamlet or village. Given that more than 90% of NABARD SHGs are women's groups, there is a special focus on encouraging women to join organizations. Although there are no explicit selection criteria relating to gender, wealth, class, or caste indicated, emphasis is placed on forming SHGs among women from the underprivileged classes.

NABARD helps its partners strengthen their capacity and provides financial support for the expansion of microfinance activities. Through various interventions and liquidity support to banks for SHG–bank linkage, NABARD also focuses on training and sensitizing partner agencies as part of its efforts to connect a greater number of SHGs to the banking system. The bank continues to provide 100% refinance assistance to banks for financing SHGs. NABARD takes pride in the fact that the SBLP is the largest microfinance scheme in the world. The programme currently enrols 140 million families and 11.9 million SHGs, with total savings of ₹47,240.48 crore as of 31 March 2022. The credit linkage is noteworthy, with 34 lakh SHGs linked to credit in fiscal year (FY) 2021–22, compared to 29 lakh groups in 2020–21, and loans amounting to ₹99,729.23 crore disbursed. As of 31 March 2022, the unpaid loan amounts to ₹1,51,051.30 crore for 67.40 lakh SHGs (an average of ₹2.24 lakh per group). Although the average ticket size is modest, the impact may be transformative, as evidenced by the numerous success stories in *Kurukshetra* (2022). The E. Shakti programme has digitized the financial and non-financial data of approximately 1.274 million SHGs to facilitate credit linkage with banks, aiming to enhance loan accessibility.

Since 1992, NABARD has supported SHG promotion, development, and credit linkage by awarding grants to farmers' clubs, NGOs, commercial banks, RRBs, primary agricultural credit societies (PACS), NGO–MFIs, SHG federations, and individual rural volunteers (IRVs). The SHG–BLP programme has been widely adopted across the nation; as a result, 118.93 lakh SHGs had opened bank accounts as of 31 March 2022. As of 31 March 2022, NABARD had provided support to 883,597 SHGs with a cumulative sanction of ₹17,585.79 lakh (Table 2.3).

Additionally, NABARD assists RRBs in carrying out their duties as self-help-group-promoting institutions (SHPIs) and offers them specialized training in the promotion, nurturing, and funding of SHGs. Due to their sizeable presence in rural areas, it also offers funds to district central cooperative banks (DCCBs) for the purpose of integrating SBLPs into their already existing economic activity. To date, NABARD has entered into 91 memoranda of understanding with banks (59 RRBs, 24 public-sector banks, and 8 state cooperative banks/DCCBs) under the Business Model Scheme, aiming to establish 190,330 joint-liability groups (JLGs) with a grant commitment of₹52.57 crore. As of 31 March 2022, a total of 42,621 JLGs have been established with cumulative financial assistance of ₹6.09 crore under the initiative.

NABARD has been using three different types of financial connection models, as listed below, with the goal of ensuring that the poor have access to formal financial institutions in mind. NABARD has also conducted training programmes and exposure trips to successful JLGs to sensitize stakeholders of the JLG programme, targeting functionaries from various institutions, including financing banks, in terms of non-financial support interventions. In total, about 92,271 individuals have benefited from these training sessions and exposure trips.

Table 2.3 Grant support to partner agencies

(₹ in lakhs)								
Agency	During 2021–22				As of 31 Mar 2022			
	Sanctions		Release		Cumulative sanctions		Cumulative release	
	Amount	SHGs promoted (no.)	Amount	SHG saving linked (no.)	Amount	SHGs promoted (no.)	Amount	SHG saving linked (no.)
NGOs	192.50	2,025	460.83	6,428	38,236.30	702,677	16,059.71	550,925
RRBs	–	–	–	–	1,764.38	61,656	666.90	55,288
Coop. banks	–	–	–	–	1,294.22	66,782	609.33	59,975
IRVs	–	–	–	–	455.18	26,350	78.25	12,313
Farmers' clubs	–	–	–	–	46.13	5,138	20.45	4,469
PACS	–	–	1.51	130	669.61	14,925	97.08	3,441
SHG federations	–	–	–	–	25.40	200	12.37	46
NGOs–MFIs	–	–	–	–	337.13	5,869	41.70	1,126
Total	**192.50**	**2,025**	**462.34**	**6,558**	**42,828.35**	**883,597**	**17,585.79**	687.583
Women SHG Scheme (in 150 left-wing extremism-affected and backward districts)								
Anchor NGOs	NA	NA	933.74	–	20,438.10	204,381	13,943	129,167

Source: Compiled by the author.

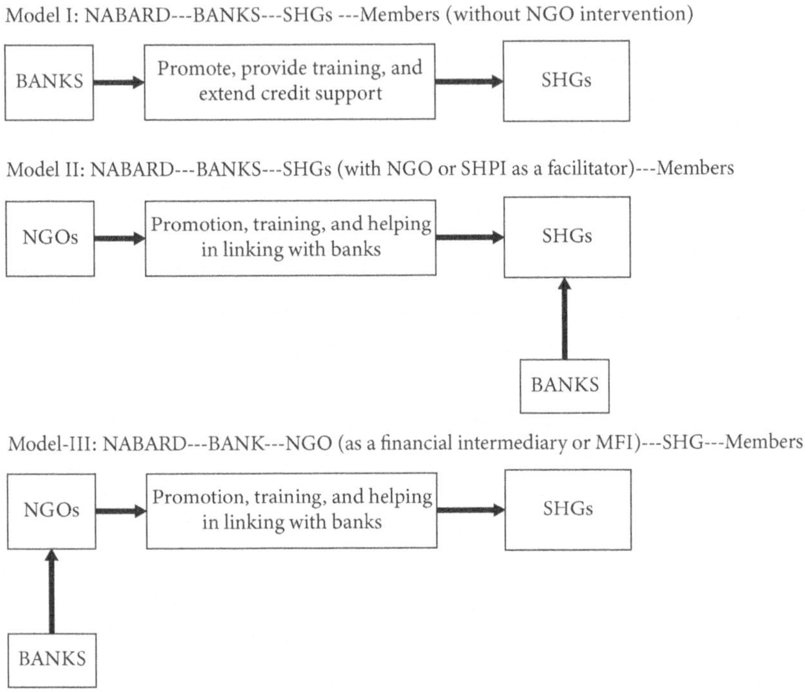

Fig. 2.1 NABARD's models of linking banks with self-help groups (SHGs)
Source: Different publications of NABARD and the RBI.

In Model I, the financing bank itself serves as an SHPI. NABARD emphasizes the training and other support services to groups through the SHPI in addition to encouraging their financial connections with banks. The bank initiates the formation of groups, nurtures them over time, opens their savings account, and then extends credit to them after determining that they are ready to accept credit. RRBs have played a significant role in developing this type of model (NABARD 1999).

Facilitating organizations such as NGOs, governmental bodies, or other community-based groups serve as SHPIs. Some of them receive direct selection and funding from NABARD, whereas other recipients receive funding from domestic or foreign donor organizations. These organizations provide assistance and education to the groups. Following the evaluation of the SHGs' operations and their capacity to manage credit, banks provide savings accounts and then extend credit directly to the SHGs. The predominant framework for linking experiences is an NGO or another organization serving as the facilitator.

The SHPIs function as a channel for financial transactions between entities and banks under Model III. In certain areas, banks are incapable of providing direct financial support to the SHGs, which are facilitated and promoted by alternative SHPIs. In these contexts, NGOs function as intermediaries in microfinance and as facilitators. Before they approach banks for substantial loans to refinance SHGs, they aid, nurture, and educate the groups. In this framework, it has been noted that NGOs consolidate the SHGs and gradually provide the SHG federations with the necessary resources to execute this role.

2.9 The Small Industries Development Bank of India (SIDBI)

The SIDBI is a prominent financial institution that facilitates the development of SHGs to promote micro-entrepreneurship. In 1994, the Micro-Credit Scheme (MCS) was created to provide financial help to MFIs so that they could lend money to poor people in rural areas, especially women, to support small businesses outside of farming. In January 1999, the bank founded the mission SIDBI Foundation for Microcredit (SFMC) subsequent to the successful completion of the MCS pilot phase. The basic goal of the SFMC is to establish a nationwide network of robust, viable, and long-lasting MFIs from both the informal and official financial sectors to offer microfinance services to the underprivileged, particularly women.

To help the retailing MFIs become financially self-sufficient organizations, the SFMC offers a wide range of financial and non-financial services, including loan funding, grant support, equity, and institution-building support. In addition to providing loan support for their micro-credit projects, the SFMC finds, develops, and supports a limited group of potential MFIs as long-term partners. Therefore, the SIDBI Foundation's qualified partner institutions include big and medium-sized MFIs with a minimum annual fund demand of ₹10 lakh. SFMC forecasts anticipate developing approximately 100–125 MFIs into long-term partners over the next 4 years.

On 31 March 2022, the SIDBI claimed that it had developed the capacity of 100+ MFIs and made a cumulative disbursement of ₹27,327 crore, impacting 49.23 million beneficiaries that constitute 96–98% women beneficiaries. The SIDIBI further documented that it has brought about changes in the livelihood pattern by giving impetus to enterprise activity.

The bank launched the Promoting Regular and Assisted Migration for Youth and Skilled Professionals (PRAYAAS) scheme to facilitate enterprise promotion and to bring down the cost of loans to BPL borrowers. On 31 March 2022, under the PRAYAAS scheme, the bank sanctioned limits to 13 Parter Institutions (PIs) (financial intermediaries, including NBFC/MFIs/fintech (11) and non-financial intermediaries (2)), out of which the limit to 10 PIs is operational. An aggregate sanction of ₹417.70 crore was approved, covering 27,343 beneficiaries, and an aggregate disbursement of ₹342.25 crore was given to 21,529 beneficiaries. Out of the total disbursed cases under PRAYAAS, approximately 88% of beneficiaries are from rural areas.

The Micro Units Development and Refinance Agency (MUDRA), a wholly owned subsidiary of the SIDBI, was established in 2015 with the goal of 'funding the unfunded'. MUDRA had sanctioned an amount of ₹15,623 crore during FY 2022 as against an amount of ₹12,312 crore. The disbursement for FY 2022 stood at ₹14,989 crore and for FY 2021 at ₹12,303 crore.

2.10 Rashtriya Mahila Kosh

The GoI established the National Credit Fund for Women, also known as Rashtriya Mahila Kosh (RMK), in March 1993. The organization was founded as a society under the Societies Registration Act 1860. RMK was established to promote assistance programmes aimed at enhancing lending facilities for low-income women for income-generating initiatives or asset accumulation. It also recognizes the role of women's organizations in socio-economic development and transformation.

RMK operates as the premier wholesaler in the business, facilitating the allocation of funds from the government and donors to retail intermediary microfinance organizations (IMOs). By providing support to new and less experienced IMOs through incentive programmes, technology help, staff training, and other services that don't involve money, it improves the availability of microfinance. Two subsequent notable programmes provide financial assistance. One programme aims to support the growth and stabilization of SHGs, referred to as support for partner MFIs that are formalizing and regulating their organizational structure to effectively manage microfinance operations. Middle-level mutual funds receive minimal operational capital assistance through a short-term lending initiative to address liquidity challenges. Grants, technical assistance, and operational support are provided to the partner MFIs to facilitate their operational expansion and achieve self-sufficiency. The programme for loan marketing is the primary loan programme revolving fund scheme, clause 14(c). The loan schemes have been structured sequentially to allow IMOs and ultimate borrowers to start with smaller loan schemes and gradually transition to larger ones as they gain expertise and expand their outreach.

By the end of March 2006, the overall number of eventual borrowers from the primary loan programme supported by RMK exceeded 3.6 lakh. Nearly 1.5 lakh and 0.25 lakh beneficiaries, respectively, fall under the revolving fund and loan promotion schemes. Along with lending programmes, RMK has extended financial assistance for housing and marketing campaigns, furthering the cause of poor and vulnerable women's social and economic uplift.

2.11 Collective financial intermediaries

Some of the leading national organizations promoting SHGs in the nation have been covered above. Aside from that, India is also home to numerous international donor organizations. These include the DFID, USAID, the World Bank, and the United Nations, which have given NGOs and MFIs a lot of resources in the form of grants or loans to promote SHGs in rural areas. Many of these organizations have started several initiatives in various states connecting SHGs with various desired goals, including the promotion of diverse livelihood methods, women's emancipation, and the reduction of poverty. Their strategies differ depending on the project requirements of the donor organizations or the SHPI approach as contextualized in the local situation.

Nevertheless, the great majority of NGOs and MFIs in India promote SHGs in general accordance with the NABARD linkage model with funding from national or international donor organizations. These NGOs include Professional Assistance for Development Action (PRADAN), MYRADA, the Social Performance Management Scheme (SPMS), and the Development for Human Action (DHAN) Foundation in Madurai, among others. Some established organizations, such as PRADAN, MYRADA, and 13 RMK, offer smaller loans, up to a maximum of ₹500,000, to encourage credit and thrift among younger, smaller, but potentially capable organizations. To qualify for this plan, the organization must possess a minimum of six months of experience in credit and savings. This initiative is evaluating 14 organizations with at least 3 years of experience in lending and saving. The maximum borrowing limit per organization is 3 crore. The initiative is also evaluating 15 organizations with a demonstrated track record and 5 years of experience in microfinance. The groups may allocate the principal amount sanctioned by RMK to the SHGs for income-generating activities. This programme allows for a maximum loan amount of ₹5 crore. With the long-term objective of turning the SHGs into institutions that can sustain themselves, it has begun to federate SHGs. While some NGOs/MFIs have opted for the Grameen model of group creation, some NGOs/MFIs, like SEWA Bank in Ahmedabad, have followed the individual cooperative approach. Community Action for Self-Help (CASH) is prominent among the latter, such as the Association for Social Advancement (ASA) Trust in Tiruchirappalli, Tamil Nadu, Organisation for Rural Reconstruction (OR)in Uttar Pradesh, Society for Helping Awakening Rural Poor through Education (SHARE) in Andhra Pradesh, etc. Naturally, this approach emphasizes the group members' joint obligation for any borrower who is a member.

2.12 Status of microcredit after NABARD took the lead in supporting SHGs

As observed in Chapter 1, microcredit to money-starved citizens is not new to India. Either the rural money lenders in the informal sectors, or credit cooperative societies, or scheduled commercial banks, or the RRBs (since 1975) and other non-banking financial institutions or MFIs (Bandhan Bank, Spandana, etc.) have been trying to fill the credit gap for micro activities. Since 1982, in addition to the existing financial institutions, NABARD has assumed the leadership role in supervising and monitoring microfinance activities in the country. However, NABARD largely focuses on delivering microcredit through SHGs and NGOs and other societies linked to SHGs. The paragraph containing Fig. 2.1 above in section 2.8 discussed the three models of NABARD's linkages with SHGs.

Tables 2.4 and 2.5 explain NABARD's support to microfinance through SHGs. These tables reveal that NABARD is predominantly supporting microcredit delivery through SHGs but not individuals, whereas the RRBs and other scheduled commercial banks in the public and private sectors are also lending for micro activities by individuals. Banks like the State Bank of India, Punjab National Bank, and RRBs are lending a minimum of ₹5,000/- to a maximum of ₹50,000/- for micro activities such as street vendors, vegetable vendors, and rural artisans. However, these banks are lending only under the coverage of Prime Minister Swarojgar Yojana or MUDRA schemes. All other microfinance activities of these banks are only through SHGs.

In addition to NABARD oversight on microfinance through SHGs, the RBI also regulates microfinance activity in the country. The RBI-regulated private financial institutions basically provide microcredit to individuals instead of SHGs. As of 31 January 2022, RBI has a list of 97 non-banking MFIs (see Annexure I) in the country functioning in the private sector. These institutions finance individuals in small amounts for their business needs. Normally, the borrowers from these institutions are artisans, small businesspersons, street vendors, professionals, and other microeconomic activities.

2.13 Microcredit by RRBs

With a view to providing institutional credit to the poor households engaged in services, small businesses, and agriculture, the Indian Government established RRBs in association with a public-sector sponsor bank and the state governments in 1975. The country's first five RRBs were formed on 2 October 1975, with a specific focus on serving the needs of small and marginal farmers, agricultural labourers, craftsmen, and poorer segments of society in terms of financial inclusion. RRBs originally focused only on microcredit.

Table 2.4 Achievements of the SBLP (31 March 2021)

S. no.	Particulars	Physical (no. in lakhs)	Amount (₹ in crores)
1	**SHGs' savings linked with banks as of 31 March 2022**	118.93	47,240.48
(i)	Exclusive women SHGs	104.00	42,104.77
(ii)	Out of the total SHGs—under the NRLM/SGSY	71.84	27,576.94
(iii)	Out of the total SHGs under the National Urban Livelihood Mission (NULM)/ Swarna Jayanti Shahari Rojgar Yojana (SJSRY)	5.81	2,600.19
2	**No. of SHGs credit linked during the year 2021–22**	33.98	99,729.22
(i)	Women SHGs	31.50	93,817.21
(ii)	SHGs—under the NRLM/SGSY	22.91	63,100.77
(iii)	SHGs—under the NULM/SJSRY	1.84	5,816.10
3	**SHGs having loans outstanding as of 31 March 2022**	67.40	151,051.30
(i)	Women SHGs	62.65	142,288.61
(ii)	SHGs—under the NRLM/SGSY	44.54	94,231.52
(iii)	SHGs—under the NULM/SJSRY	3.27	7,608.57
4	**Avg. credit outstanding/SHG on 31 March 2022**		2.24
5	**Mean credit disbursed/SHG during 2021–22 (in ₹)**		2.93
6	**Families covered up to 31 March 2022**	1,419.44	
7	**Banks and financial institutions submitted Management Information System (MIS) (no.)**	344	
8	**Details of JLGs**		
(i)	JLG (31 March 2021)	133.83	213,164.88
(ii)	JLGs promoted during 2021–22	54.09	112,772.75
(iii)	Cumulative JLGs promoted up to 31 March 2022	187.92	325,937.63
9	**NABARD's support**		
(i)	Capacity development of partner institutions		
	Under SHG-BLP and JLGs		
	No. of programmes conducted during 2021–22 (in no. only)	5,383	
	No. of participants attending during 2021–22 (in lakhs)	2.93	

Table 2.4 Continued

S. no.	Particulars	Physical (no. in lakhs)	Amount (₹ in crores)
	Total no. of participants trained up to 31 March 2022 (in lakhs)	45.42	
	Under the Women's Self-Help Group (WSHG) Scheme (in left-wing extremism-affected and backward districts)		
	No. of programmes conducted during 2021–22 (in no. only)	1,250	
	No. of participants covered during 2021–22 (in lakhs)	0.6	
(ii)	Refinance extended to banks during 2021–22		10,187.40
	Total refinance up to 31 March 2022		101,019.21
(iii)	**Revolving fund assistance (RFA) and capital support to MFIs**		
	RFA outstanding as of 31 March 2022		3.61
	Capital support outstanding as of 31 March 2022		3.59
	Refinance extended to NBFC–MFIs during 2021–22		16,451.39
(iv)	**Grant provided to SHPIs for promotion of SHGs under SHG–BLP**		
	Grant sanctioned during 2021–22		10.06
	Cumulative sanctioned up to 31 March 2022		428.28
(v)	Cumulative grants sanctioned to anchor NGOs for promotion of SHGs under the WSHG Development Scheme up to 31 March 2022		418.22
(vi)	Cumulative grant to Joint Liability Group Promoting Institutions (JLGPIs) for promotion of Joint Liability Groups (JLGs up to 31 March 2022		255.81

Source: Compiled by the author from various RBI and NABARD documents.

RRBs have changed greatly in the nearly 50 years since their founding, but they have stayed loyal to their mission of servicing the target group outlined in the RRBs Act 1976's preamble. The priority sector receives 90% of their overall loan portfolio, with 92% of their 21,892 branches located in rural or semi-urban areas. The percentage of their overall loan portfolio that goes to small and marginal farmers and the weaker sectors

Table 2.5 Progress made under the SBLP (2017–18 to 2021–22) (no. in lakhs/₹ in crores)

Particulars		2017–18		2018–19		2019–20		2020–21		2021–22	
		No. of SHGs	Amount	No. of SHGs	Amount	No. of SHGs	Amount	No. of SHGs	Amount	No. of SHGs	Amount
SHG saving deposits in banks as of 31 March	Total SHG nos	87.44 (1.95%)	19,592.12 (21.59%)	100.14 (14.52%)	23,324.48 (19.05%)	102.43 (2.29%)	26,152.05 (12.12%)	112.23 (9.57%)	37,477.61 (43.31%)	118.93 (5.97%)	47,240.48 (26.05%)
	All women SHGs	73.90 (0.94%)	17,497.86 (22.51%)	85.31 (15.44%)	20,473.55 (17.01%)	88.32 (3.53%)	23,320.55 (13.91%)	97.25 (10.11%)	32,686.08 (40.16%)	104.05 (6.99%)	42,104.77 (28.81%)
	Percentage of women	84.51	89.31	85.19	87.78	86.22	89.17	86.65	87.21	87.45	89.13
	Of which NRLM/SGSY	41.84 (11.76%)	10,434.03 (38.15%)	55.80 (33.37%)	12,867.18 (23.32%)	57.89 (3.75%)	14,312.7 (11.23%)	64.78 (11.9%)	19,353.7 (35.22%)	71.84 (10.89%)	27,576.94 (42.49%)
	Percentage of NRLM/SGSY groups	47.85	53.26	55.72	55.17	56.52	54.73	57.72	51.64	60.40	58.38
	Of which NULM/SJSRY	4.25 (−22.10%)	1,350.80 (19.87%)	4.39 (3.29%)	1,614.42 (19.52%)	4.69 (6.83%)	1,523.57 (−5.63%)	5.29 (12.79%)	1,954.09 (28.26%)	5.81 (9.87%)	2,600.19 (33.06%)
	Percentage of NULM/SJSRY groups	4.86	6.89	4.38	6.92	4.58	5.83	4.71	5.21	4.89	5.50

Credit disbursed to SHGs during the year	No. of SHGs obtaining credit	22.61 (19.13%)	47,185.88 (21.67%)	26.98 (19.33%)	58,317.63 (23.59%)	31.46 (16.60%)	77,659.35 (33.17%)	28.87 (−8.23%)	58,070.68 (−25.22%)	33.98 (17.71%)	99,729.22 (71.74%)
	All women SHGs	20.75 (20.92%)	44,558.74 (23.42%)	23.65 (13.98%)	53,254.04 (19.51%)	28.84 (21.95%)	73,297.56 (37.64%)	25.9 (−10.19%)	54,423.13 (−25.75%)	31.50 (21.63%)	93,817.21 (72.38%)
	Percentage of women groups	91.78	94.43	87.66	91.32	91.67	94.38	89.71	93.72	92.70	94.07
	Of which NRLM/SGSY	12.70 (43.41%)	25,055.18 (44.52%)	16.49 (29.84%)	33,398.93 (33.30%)	20.49 (24.26%)	52,183.73 (56.24%)	15.84 (−22.69%)	29,643.04 (−43.19%)	22.91 (44.64%)	63,100.77 (112.87%)
	Percentage of NRLM/SGSY groups	56.20	53.10	61.12	57.27	65.13	67.20	54.87	51.05	67.42	63.27
	Of which NULM/SJSRY	1.06 (0.17%)	2,424.07 (−9.41%)	1.29 (21.70%)	3,419.58 (41.07%)	1.59 (23.26%)	3,406.22 (−0.39%)	1.13 (−28.93%)	2,112.04 (−37.99%)	1.84 (62.45%)	5,816.10 (175.38%)
	Percentage of NULM/SJSRY groups	4.71	5.14	4.78	5.86	5.05	4.39	3.91	3.63	5.40	5.83
Credit outstanding from SHGs as of 31 March	No. of SHGs linked	50.20 (3.55%)	75,598.45 (22.76%)	50.77 (1.14%)	87,098.15 (15.21%)	56.77 (11.82%)	108,075.07 (24.08%)	57.8 (1.81%)	103,289.71 (−4.43%)	67.40 (16.61%)	151,051.30 (46.24%)
	No. of women-only SHGs linked	45.49 (6.20%)	70,401.73 (24.73%)	44.61 (−1.93%)	79,231.98 (12.54%)	51.12 (14.59%)	100,620.71 (27.00%)	53.11 (3.89%)	96,596.6 (−4.00%)	62.65 (17.96%)	142,288.61 (47.30%)

(continued)

Table 2.5 Continued

Particulars	2017–18		2018–19		2019–20		2020–21		2021–22	
	No. of SHGs	Amount	No. of SHGs	Amount	No. of SHGs	Amount	No. of SHGs	Amount	No. of SHGs	Amount
Percentage of women SHGs	90.62	93.13	87.87	90.97	90.05	93.10	91.89	93.52	92.95	94.20
Of which NRLM/SGSY	27.93 (12.13%)	38,225.29 (27.44%)	32.85 (17.62%)	54,320.91 (42.11%)	36.89 (12.30%)	67,717.07 (24.66%)	33.78 (–8.43%)	57,336.62 (–15.33%)	44.54 (31.87%)	94,231.52 (64.35%)
Percentage of NRLM/SGSY groups to total	55.63	50.56	64.70	62.37	64.98	62.66	58.44	55.51	66.09	62.38
Of which NULM/SJSRY	2.90 (–8.58%)	5350.63 (29.45%)	2.25 (–22.41%)	4,110.73 (–23.17)	2.67 (18.67%)	5,466.87 (32.99%)	2.23 (–16.48%)	4,056.45 (–25.8%)	3.27 (46.52%)	7,608.57 (87.57%
Percentage of NULM/SJSRY groups to total	5.79	7.08	4.43	4.72	4.70	5.06	3.86	3.93	4.85=	5.04

Note: The figures in brackets indicate the increase *or* decrease over the previous year.

Source: Compiled by the author from the data from various RBI and NABARD documents.

is 48% and 60%, respectively. However, RRBs' shift towards non-priority and urban financing is documented.

The merger of RRBs, which reduced the number from 196 in FY 2004–05 to 43 as of 3 March 2022, has improved scale efficiency, increased productivity, and strengthened RRBs' financial standing. In FY 2021–22, RRBs have performed admirably. With several RRBs reporting net profit after around five years of straight losses, the consolidated net profit climbed by 91% to ₹3,219 crore. However, some RRBs' use of information technology and the nine banks reporting losses continually are of concern. Pension liabilities and declining asset quality have negatively impacted these banks.

During the initial days of RRBs, they were the gamechangers in the rural economy by bringing the rural businesspeople, agricultural labourers, and farmers from the clutches of rural money lenders. They opened branches in remote and inaccessible rural areas all over the country. As of 31 March 2022, RRBs have extended microcredit to the tune of ₹21,861,825.26 lakh to 19,304,959 borrowers. People of weaker sections are treated as microcredit borrowers.

2.14 The state-run MFI's approach to microfinance

A new era in the provision of banking services to the underprivileged has begun as a result of the rapid expansion of branch networks in the RRBs, other scheduled commercial banks, and cooperative sectors in rural areas. Even though these banks have assisted rural India in the socio-economic development of the poor, a significant portion of the impoverished population still struggles to obtain necessary credit from the banking sector. The SHG–Bank Linkage initiative, which was introduced to the nation in 1992 under the auspices of NABARD, marked the beginning of inclusive development. Credit flow for consumption and other productive uses has increased significantly as a result of SHG formation and their relationship with banks. However, for a variety of reasons, the poor can be unable to obtain sufficient and timely financing. As a result, they are turning to high-cost credit offered by moneylenders, moneylending institutions, or MFIs. Consequently, a cycle of debt ensnared some impoverished individuals in the former state of Andhra Pradesh, leading to cases of suicide. In 2010, the state government enacted a law regulating MFI activity within the state. Despite significant demand for loans, the banking sector was incapable of providing sufficient quantities. In compliance with the State Cooperative Societies Act of 1964, the state government established the Credit Cooperative Federation in partnership with Mandal Samakhyas and Pattana Samakhyas and registered it on 7 September 2011.

Its aims are to augment the banking sector's credit assistance promptly and economically by providing credit to SHG members and to alleviate poverty through the financing of income-generating enterprises. The goal is to promote the socio-economic development of participants in SHGs, both in rural and urban environments (Unique Qualities 2.5). The state-run MFI (SRMFI) has shown strong growth over the past six years and has become a significant help to the impoverished in both urban and rural areas across the state. Currently, because credit is timely and reasonably priced, the poor do not need to look anywhere other than the SRMFI to obtain it for their urgent and livelihood-related needs. The following characteristics set the SRMFI apart from other players in the microfinance industry: timely loan in forty-eight hours and at a cheap cost; strong community stake in ownership and administration; collaboration with state government; low operational costs since SHG federations under an agency framework provide last-mile connection; easy product modification based on community demands; a transparent and user-friendly IT platform for operations as a channelling agency, facilitating the correct implementation of government programmes; support to the SBLP to ensure credit discipline to reduce non-performing assets (NPAs) as credit is only extended to regular SHGs under the SBLP; strengthening SHG federations financially and operationally through rating and service fee payments; ensuring social security through risk mitigation services to members; promoting financial inclusion as business correspondent to banks and extending Me Seva services (government to citizen services); and earmarking credit to SC, ST, and Poorest of the Poor (PoP) members; promoting livelihood and income-generating activities with a focus on financing (Fig. 2.2).

The SRMFI is different from other MFIs. The differences are identified in Table 2.6.

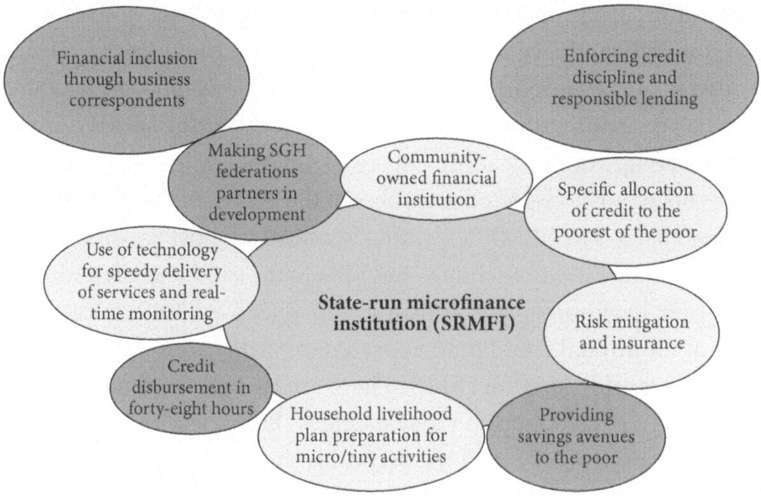

Fig. 2.2 The functioning of SRMFIs

Source: Prepared by the author with inputs from Stree Nidhi MFI Annual Report 2017–18.

Table 2.6 SRMFIs versus other MFIs

SRMFI	Other MFIs
• Community-owned • SHG federations – last mile connectivity • Needs-based lending • Low operational cost at 1–2% of the working capital • Low interest rates—13% to members • Margin shared with village-level organization and Mandal Samakhya (MS) at 1.25% and 0.25% each • No processing charges levied • No profit motive • Holistic approach to poverty alleviation • No unhealthy practices in recovery • Transparency in functioning • Concern for the poor while being self-sustainable	• Promoted by private individuals' organizations • Lending using only employees • High operational costs at 8–10% of the working capital • High interest rates—21% • 1% processing charges levied • Lending through JLGs • No holistic approach to poverty alleviation • No transparency in functioning • Business-orientated

Source: Compiled by the author from different sources.

In addition to the above differences, the unique feature of the SRMFI is that it identified the consumption needs of some of the borrowers and extended financial support in addition to finance for economic activities. The major consumption requirements supported by the SRMFI are the health, marriage, and educational needs of members. However, such support has been only to selected members of the SHGs and purely declared on a needs basis. The SRMFI extended financial support to consumption needs under the Suvidha scheme. Suvidha loans can be availed for both lower-order livelihoods and consumption purposes but are restricted to 35% of the annual credit plan allocated to a village-level organization (VO)/slum-level federation (SLF). There are two schemes under which the SRMFI gives consumption loans. One is the Society for Elimination of Rural Poverty (SERP), and the second is the Mission for Elimination of Poverty in Municipal Areas (MEPMA).

As per Table 2.7, only 6.06% of borrowers are provided with consumption loans under various schemes of the SRMFI, and about 4.07% of the total loan portfolio goes to consumption loans, leaving behind a sizeable 94% of the borrowers outside the schemes of granting consumption loans (loans for marriages, education, and health).

Looking at the social spending behaviour of the population in India, social and other consumption needs include education, health, marriage, fares, festivals, births, deaths, poojas, visits of relations near and far, and inviting the married girl child home once in a while and treating them. None of the loans factor in the money required for these activities.

This chapter can be summed up thus: this phenomenon is not unprecedented. For decades, policymakers have recognized the role of rural

Table 2.7 Consumption loans by SRMFIs

(₹ in crores)				
	Consumption loans		All loans	
	Members	Amount	Members	Amount
SERP	22,893	89.00	400,837	2,360.94
MEPMA	9,034	36.00	124,902	708.28
Total	**31,927**	**125.00**	**525,739**	**3,069.22**

Source: Compiled by the author from SRMFI annual reports.

moneylenders, who offer emergency credit to the poor while utilizing exploitative recovery tactics and charging exorbitant interest. It was this concept that led to the establishment of RRBs in India way back in 1975—'to save the rural poor from the firm grip of money lenders'. MFIs have been primarily made to believe that they came about as a tool to alleviate poverty by creating more employment opportunities for the small and medium enterprise (SME) sector, better health-care systems, and extending small and trouble-free credit to the poorer section of society for their immediate business and social needs. But what we see today is the opposite—cumbersome processes in obtaining loans, security, and guarantees linked to microcredits, although it is not the policy of microlending; very high interest rates; slower growth rates; fewer employment opportunities; highly indebted rural and urban poor; and resultant unending subsistence poverty. The underlying question is to what extent these MFIs have had an effect on mainstreaming the poor into economic policies—whether it is a menace or a reassurance for the poor. However, that concept or philosophy no longer exists as RRBs moved to more lucrative business centres, giving in to the lobbying strengths of a new cult of licensed moneylenders who christened themselves microfinanciers. Later, NABARD was created in 1982 in furtherance of the philosophy of RRBs and to streamline microfinance.

Thus, the microfinance concept started to grow with government endeavours to engage itself in financing the poor and later with the involvement of the private sector by setting up MFIs; however, the concept of public-sector microcredit was sold to the private sector at the cost of state-sponsored RRBs.

The microcredit sector, with the participation of the private sector, witnessed continuous growth from 2006 onwards. The industry for microlenders has grown for FY 2015, thus registering a quantum jump in loans given and the number of new MFIs.

The microloans/microcredit in the country grew by nearly 11% to ₹71,916 crore during the second quarter of the current financial year (2022–23). Microloans worth ₹64,899 crore were released during the same period.

In terms of number of credit accounts, a total of 1.81 crore loans were released during quarter 2 (Q2) FY 2022–23, as against 1.85 crore loans in Q2 FY 2021–22, as per the 2022–23 report by the Microfinance

Institutions Network (MFIN). According to the—Q2 FY 2022–23 report, the country's microfinance loan portfolio stood at over₹3 lakh crore at the end of September 2022, serving 6.2 crore unique borrowers with 12 crore loan accounts: 'As of September 30, 2022, the microfinance industry possesses a total gross loan portfolio of ₹3,00,974 crore', a year-on-year gain of 235% above ₹2,43,737 crore as of 30 September 2021, the report stated. 'Thirteen banks hold the highest part of 377% of the total outstanding microloans, at ₹1,13,565 crore. NBFC-MFIs are the second largest provider of microcredit, with an outstanding credit of ₹1,10,418 crore, representing 36.7% of the overall sector portfolio.'

The average loan disbursed per account for the quarter was ₹40,571, reflecting an increase of approximately 12% compared to the corresponding quarter of FY 2021–22. Small financing banks (SFBs) have an outstanding loan amount of ₹50,029 crore, representing a stake of 166%. NBFCs represent 79%, while other MFIs comprise 1.1% of the microfinance sector.

The data said that active microfinance loan accounts rose by 142% over the preceding 12 months, reaching 12 crore as of 30 September 2022. The eastern, northeastern, and southern regions comprised 63.9% of the overall portfolio. Tamil Nadu has the largest outstanding portfolio among the states, followed by Bihar and West Bengal. In Q2 FY 23, the microfinance sector reached an outstanding portfolio of ₹3,00,974 crore. NBFC–MFIs have also collectively crossed the ₹1 lakh crore mark, though banks still have the majority share in the microfinance market.

'The CAGR of the industry in the past five years has been a healthy 22.2% despite two years of disruption due to the pandemic', said Alok Misra, Chief Executive Officer (CEO) and Director, MFIN (Economic Times 2023). Microfinance industry body MFIN is an RBI-recognized self-regulatory organization. He made this statement in December 2022 following the release of the MFIN Micrometre report for Q2 FY 2022–23. The data highlighted the resilience of India's microfinance sector, which had reached a portfolio milestone of over ₹3 lakhs crore despite the economic challenges posed by the COVID-19 pandemic of 2020. The growth momentum is likely to pick up further, as the estimated credit demand is expected to be ₹17–20 lakh crore by 2025, Alok Misra added (Economic Times 2023).

The trends further suggest that the public-sector MFIs (RRBs) established by the government to alleviate poverty in rural areas have today turned commercial. They gave way to moneylenders getting licences to lend and drawing credit from public-sector banks. According to M. Yunus, a well-known guru of microfinance by private players, 'These small loans would generate income, and the poor clients would be able to repay the loans' (Yunus 1999). Today, the story is different—the poor are thrown into poverty after taking the loans from MFIs.

The poor are trapped in a vicious debt cycle—they take loans to start small businesses, they cannot compete with big business houses, they become unable to repay the instalments, they fail to pay the interest at which they borrowed, so they again take loans to pay back old loans from other institutions, and the cycle goes on. The interest charged by well-known institutes that are often discussed as successful is sometimes as high as 36% per year flat, plus administrative and processing fees, with collateral not mentioned again.

To this, Banerjee, Duflo, Pranab, and Bardhan argued that 'when it works well, microfinance can be a win-win situation, as the poor can borrow money at rates that may look high but are much lower than those offered by moneylenders, and banks can make a sustainable business in lending to the poor' (Banerjee et al. 2010). This statement ignores the fact that the poor are trapped in debt, and the micro amounts cannot generate the money to repay. When the money was repaid, it was not always from the income generated through small investments but from something else—either a loan from another source or the sale of whatever assets they had owned.

The authors further say, 'MFIs need to be more diligent in their lending and screen borrowers better—if too many borrowers can't repay their loans, the social obligation will start to fall apart' (Banerjee et al. 2010). The question remains that microfinance loans are coupled with high interest rates, which makes the poor lender default on repaying the loans. The MFIs are very clever in selecting their beneficiaries and identifying their needs. They select the richest of the poor who can afford collateral security, a guarantee, and who are averse to social stigma. Then they lend them in small amounts, recover them with heavy interest in instalments, increase the amount next time, and next time slowly throw them into a debt trap. Thus, MFIs in India have now grown as all-India-presence institutions with thousands of branches and billions of rupees of business.

Rani, a client of a leading MFI in India hailing from the suburbs of Warangal town, summarizes by saying 'Loans from banks are always better because nobody will coerce us for repayment delays of one or two days, and their interest too is lower…We lost more than what we gained in borrowing from this MFI' (Gargi Rao, 2015). Another example quotes a woman borrower saying that 'Microfinance brings happiness in the beginning, tension at the end' (2015). This shows that MFIs 'force' their clients to repay on time, which puts pressure on the lender, thus resulting in taking more loans to repay old loans and falling into a poverty trap and contingent poverty.

Microfinance camouflages like the silver lining to a dark cloud. Economists, politicians, and NGO activists believe that it will generate an alternative economy and eliminate poverty, but they forget the real consequences in the long run. Experts say that microloans are coupled with interest rates that are higher than the bank rates and coercive recovery practices. The menaces inherent in MFIs include high interest rates, poor governance, lack of transparency, vicious debt cycles, poverty traps, and debt traps.

The harsh truth is that the new government, which promised good governance to the people, instead of ending the menace of MFIs has created a MUDRA Bank to refinance the microfinanciers and transfer small amounts from the poor to public-sector banks through Pradhan Mantri Jan Dhan Yojana (PMJDY).

When compared to other loans given by banks in both the urban and the rural areas (particularly for housing, purchase of cars, machinery, and equipment of big businesses), the rates of interest on microloans are very high. This high interest rate could be one reason why microloan borrowers are unable to repay their loans on time. Although non-repayment of microloans is not the intention of this work, it is directly linked to diversion of funds to other activities instead of income-generation activities. Generating enough income, reinvestment, meeting family needs, social needs, and repayment of loan instalments with very high interest rates is an unachievable task for the borrowers of microloans.

The Bloomberg Report of 3 May 2022 entitled 'Big Money Backs Tiny Loans That Lead to Debt, Despair and Even Suicide' (Finch et al. 2022) states,

> A wave of suicides in India a decade ago challenged the idea that micro-lending might eradicate poverty, but today's more modest goal of financial inclusion, an attempt to reach people without access to the banking system, is no less fraught. The expansion of the loosely regulated business—all those loans added up to $160 billion in 2020, about twice the amount 11 years earlier, according to industry estimates—has

resulted in millions of new borrowers for whom the dream of inclusion has turned into a nightmare of debt.

2.15 Growing NPAs

Another trend plaguing the MFIs is the growing NPAs. According to the Master Circular of the Reserve Bank of India (RBI/2012-13/64 UBD. BPD.(PCB) MC No. 3/09.14.000/2012-13, dated 14 July 2012), an asset becomes non-performing when it ceases to generate income for the bank.

Table 2.8 shows that out of a total of ₹145,200 crore, loans were disbursed to 42,955,221 SHGs in India at the rate of ₹338,027 on average to each of the SHGs, who in turn lent this amount to their members in small amounts for small businesses. Out of this, an amount of ₹5,249 crore of loans went bad and became NPAs of the bank. This non-performance of ₹5,249 crore could have an impact on the performance of not only the MFIs but also the SHGs that receive money from MFIs and distribute it among their members.

The volume of NPAs held by a nation's banks significantly influences the operation, profitability, and performance of its banking system. The bank's effectiveness can be assessed through various financial ratios, including operating ratios, profitability ratios, and liquidity ratios (Halkos and Salamouris 2004; Kumbirai and Webb, 2010; Yeh 1996). The financial performance of a bank is typically assessed using the net profit ratio (NPR), return on assets (ROA), return on equity (ROE), and net interest margin. Liquidity risk is evaluated through the liquidity ratio, while the capital adequacy ratio indicates the bank's solvency position. A significantly elevated gross NPA (GNPA) ratio indicates the inferior quality of the bank's assets, whereas a high net NPA (NNPA) functions as an indicator of the bank's overall stability. NPAs in the loan portfolio adversely affect operating performance, subsequently disrupting the profitability, liquidity, and solvency of cooperative banks (Michael 2006; Purbaningsih and Fatimah 2014). Various studies demonstrate that credit risk significantly negatively impacts profitability and liquidity (Ruziqa 2013). The studies examine the positive correlation between bank liquidity and capital adequacy, the proportion of non-performing loans, and interest rates on loans and interbank transactions (Vodova 2011) (Fig. 2.3 and Table 2.9).

Table 2.8 Institution-wise loans and NPAs (31 March 2023)

₹

Category of agency	Total savings of SHGs with banks as at 31 March 2023		Loan disbursed to SHGs by banks during 2022–23		Total outstanding bank loans against SHGs as at 31 March 2023		NPAs as at 31 March 2023	
	No. of SHGs (savings)	Savings amount	No. of SHGs (disbursed)	Loans disbursed	No. of SHGs (outstanding)	Loan outstanding	Amount of gross NPA	NPA (%)
Commercial banks	7,753,137	3,468,997.61	2,471,417	9,308,819.17	4,202,133	12,924,408.8	340,220.81	2.63
Percentage share	57.85	58.9	57.53	64.11	60.4	68.72	64.81	–
RRBs	4,047,836	1,820,277.34	1,570,469	4,429,041.17	2,193,119	4,821,593.92	119,371.64	2.48
Percentage share	30.2	30.91	36.56	30.5	31.52	25.64	22.74	–
Cooperative banks	1,602,110	599,992.61	253,635	782,162.99	561,799	1,061,877.04	65,341.36	6.15
Percentage share	11.95	10.19	5.9	5.39	8.08	5.65	12.45	–
Total	**13,403,083**	**5,889,267.56**	**4,295,521**	**14,520,023.33**	**6,957,051**	**18,807,979.77**	**524,933.81**	**2.79**

Source: NABARD, *Annual Report 2022–23* (Mumbai: NABARD).

Table 2.9 Percentage region-wise NPA level during 2022 and 2023

		(Lakhs)			
S. no.	Region	2021-22		2022-23	
		GNPA amount	NPA as a percentage of loan o/s	GNPA amount	NPA as a percentage of loan o/s
1	Northern region	18,094	10.94	15,694	7.48
2	North-eastern region	27,458	11.62	22,486	5.76
3	Eastern region	118,293	3.35	100,010	2.50
4	Central region	63,650	19.57	49,739	9.71
5	Western region	38,566	8.58	35,396	5.15
6	Southern region	308,310	2.96	301,608	2.32
	All-India	**574,371**	**3.80**	**524,933**	**2.79 (say 2.8)**

Note: During 2022–23, NPAs under bank credit to the SHGs segment witnessed a decline. GNPAs declined to 2.8% (year-on-year) of the total credit outstanding of ₹1,88,078.80 crore as of 31 March 2023 from 3.8% as of 31 March 2022 (Table 2.9). A decrease in NPAs can be seen across all regions during the year 2022–23. The absolute level of NPAs reduced in all regions, amounting to an overall decline of 9% from ₹5,743.71 crore during FY 2021–22 to ₹5,249.33 crore during FY 2022–23. A region-wise comparison of NPAs explains that the eastern and southern regions continue to have NPA levels below the all-India average. During FY 2022–23, the percentage of NPAs is the highest in the central region at 9.71%, followed by the northern region (7.48%) and the north-eastern region (5.76%).

Source: Compiled by the author from RBI and NABARD annual reports.

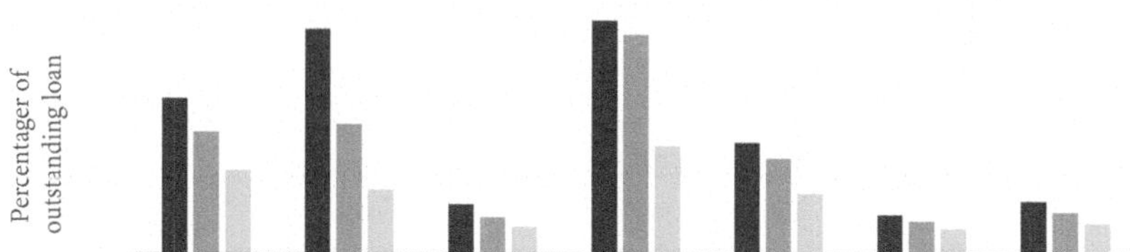

	Northern region	North-east region	Eastern region	Central region	Western region	Southern region	Pan-India
■ 2020–21	13.93	20.07	4.47	20.83	10.01	3.52	4.73
■ 2021–22	10.94	11.62	3.35	19.57	8.58	2.96	3.8
■ 2022–23	7.48	5.76	2.5	9.71	5.45	2.32	2.79

■ 2020–21 ■ 2021–22 ■ 2022–23

Fig. 2.3 Region-wise NPAs as a percentage of loan outstanding

Source: Created by the author with the data from NABARD's annual reports on microcredit.

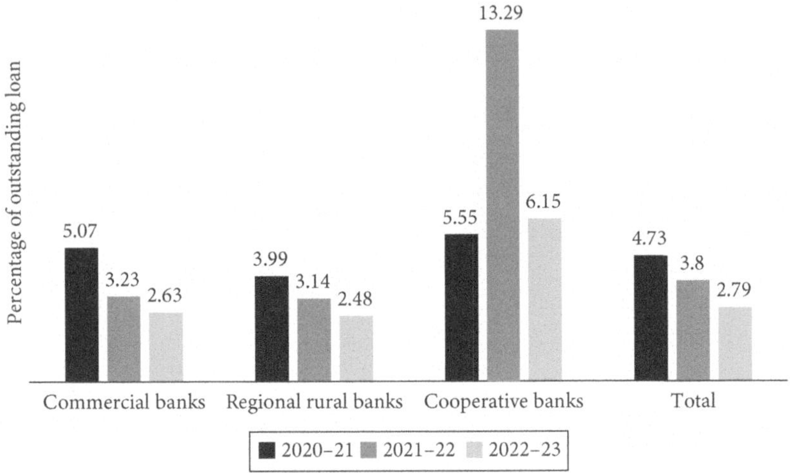

Fig. 2.4 NPA position of banks (SHG–BLP) as a percentage during the period 2020–21 to 2022–23
Source: Created by the author with data obtained from the RBI and NABARD annual reports.

Table 2.10 Lender-wise NPA as a percentage of total disbursals

Institution	2019–20	2020–21	2021–22	2022–23
NBFC–MFIs	2.23	9.45	9.10	8.47
Banks	2.36	9.45	14.39	13.82
SFBs	2.49	16.64	12.80	11.17
NBFCs	11.25	10.48	5.37	3.17
MFIs not seeking profits	3.09	9.76	9.55	9.71
Total	3.99	10.77	11.60	10.31

Source: Compiled by the author from data from NABARD and other sources.

It is worthwhile to observe NPA trends in agency-wise comparison, which reveals that NPAs reduced across commercial banks, RRBs, and rural cooperative banks (RCBs) during FY 2022–23, with the reduction being significant in the case of cooperative banks from the NPA level of 13.29% as of 31 March 2022 to 6.15% as of 31 March 2023 (Fig. 2.4).

The lender-wise NPAs given here make us think that there are institution-specific non-performances requiring independent research focusing on that institution and comparing them with other institutions that have lesser levels of NPAs.

At the onset of FY 2020–21, the Indian economy faced a substantial difficulty due to a statewide lockdown enacted in response to the sudden onset of the COVID-19 epidemic. The microfinance sector also faced negative impacts. The sector's total NPAs escalated to 10.8% by the end of March 2021, up from 4% at the end of March 2020. By the end of March 2022, they had decreased to 11.60% year-over-year. The GNPAs declined to 10.31% by the conclusion of March 2023.

A reduction in NPAs has been noted nationally, decreasing from 3.80% in FY 2021–22 to 2.79% in FY 2022–23. The agency-specific NPA levels reveal that RRBs exhibited the minimal GNPA at 2.48%, followed by other scheduled commercial banks at 2.79% and cooperative banks at 6.15%. The states of Southern India have demonstrated superior resilience to shocks, exhibiting a GNPA of 2.32%, in contrast to the central region and northern region, which report GNPAs of 9.71% and 7.28%, respectively. The commendable performance of the states of Southern India can be attributed to the presence of effective SHPIs/partner agencies and the unwavering support of proactive state governments for the SBLP. Regional disparities can be mitigated by addressing dormant accounts, cleansing data from inactive holders, overseeing the record-keeping processes of SHGs, and prioritizing a capacity-building model with active participation from state governments and banks (Fig. 2.5).

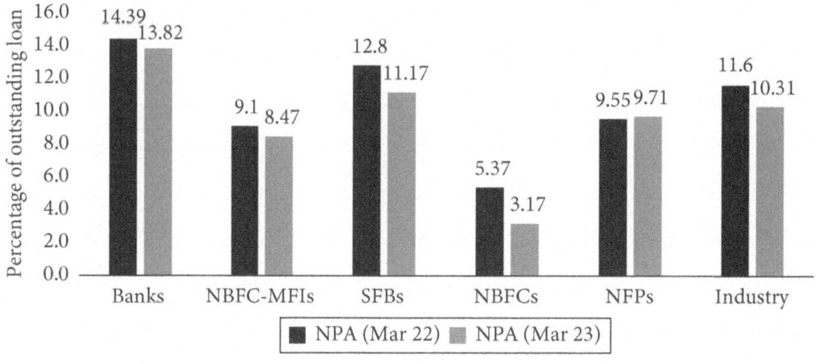

Fig. 2.5 NPA position of lenders (SHG–BLP) as a percentage during the period 2020–21 to 2022–23

Source: Compiled by the author with the data from NABARD and RBI documents.

Furthermore, Table 2.10 demonstrates that, aside from a slight decrease in 2022–23, the NPA of banks has been increasing annually, while the NPA of NBFCs has been decreasing over the years. This clearly demonstrates that private-sector NBFCs prioritize profit and business objectives, while public-sector banks emphasize social responsibilities related to poverty alleviation for their target borrowers. NPAs of not-for-profit (NFP) MFIs have shown an increasing trend, indicating that borrowers involved in micro activities are inadequately generating revenue to repay loans taken; rather, the funds have been diverted for unintended uses instead of income generation. The decrease in NPAs among NBFCs does not indicate that the borrower has effectively generated income to service the loan. The rigorous recovery protocols enacted by the NBFCs, along with the recovery strategies articulated by specific borrowers during site visits, are sometimes regarded as inhumane; thus, assets are liquidated to settle debts to maintain social standing.

3
The Perspectives of Others

3.1 Introduction

This chapter presents a review of what others have said on microfinance and its role in poverty reduction, women's empowerment, and economic development across different contexts. The studies reviewed span India, Bangladesh, Pakistan, Africa, and Latin America, highlighting both achievements and limitations of microcredit. Again, the terms 'microfinance' and 'microcredit' are used interchangeably, although microfinance covers a broader area.

3.2 What others have said

Microfinance institutions (MFIs) are often seen by the aid practitioners as transparently effective means of improving the position of the poor. There is an abundance of literature available today on microfinance. The studies reveal many impact evaluations that look at the success of MFIs in helping and aiding the poor for better economic outcomes. Most of these studies have been conducted in developing countries. Also, little is known about the effectiveness of targeting the 'core poor', which is a major flaw in Spandana, a microfinance institution's intervention. However, keeping in view the wider area of microfinance knowledge and the limited scope of this work, the book focuses here on some relevant previous studies. Moreover, it is the general perception and belief that social responsibilities, cultural rituals, traditions, customs, festivals, etc. play a very important and culture-sensitive role in the lives of many who are in financial need. These events even decide the quantum of credit requirements and expenditure patterns of borrowers from MFIs.

Microcredit Misallocation? P. Gargi Rao, Oxford University Press. © P. Gargi Rao 2026.
DOI: 10.1093/9780197910573.003.0003

Here, I examine the work that throws light on microfinance by Banerjee and Duflo (2009), which looked at a randomized control trial of microfinance implemented in Hyderabad, India. In their paper, Banerjee and Duflo (2009) looked at the impact of microfinance on various issues, such as expenditure on health, education, setting up new businesses, women's participation.

The programme in Hyderabad does not mandate microloans to be spent on businesses; moreover, the spending pattern of the household is not monitored by the MFI. Although the conventional motivation for the household to take up the loans was to start a business, this was not mentioned specifically when the experiment was conducted; hence, it is a form of randomized control trial. Briefly, this paper showed that microfinance did help the poor households to overcome the shocks of health and improve school facilities, but it did not lead to supporting a greater increase in expenditure for health care or better health outcomes for children, and neither were there any scarring effects on education as a whole. Nor does the study by Banerjee and Duflo (2009), which looks closely at the expenditure by the households on social events and cultural commitments.

In parts, this work evaluates the existing literature on microfinance and its impact on health, education and social commitments, social events, and traditions in light of how much households spend when microloans are provided.

At the global level, strengthening health systems and giving priorities to health indicators is one of the tools to measure achievement of poverty reduction. Many MFIs are now inclined towards achieving better health outcomes and reducing poverty. Numerous impact evaluation studies support the effectiveness of microfinance and its impact on poverty. Research funded by the World Bank examined the impact of three MFIs in Bangladesh over a seven-year period and found dramatic decreases in overall poverty, with the highest impact on those families in extreme poverty. To this, Leatherman and Dunford (2010) added that 'However, microfinance is not a silver bullet; legitimate issues exist, such as the ability to address the needs of extremely poor people, the level of debt burden for individuals, and the uneven performance of microfinance institutions worldwide.'

A small but growing number of studies show that the MFIs are capable of contributing to health improvement. Dunford (2001), in his paper, looked at the integration of microfinance with the promotion of family planning/birth control and combating HIV/AIDS in Bolivia and Uganda. He showed that there has been a positive impact on the health situation by creating awareness about HIV/AIDS. Pronyk and colleagues (2006) found that microfinance is associated with reduced risk of physical or sexual abuse in South Africa. In Ghana, de la Cruz and colleagues found that MFIs could effectively contribute to community and national malaria initiatives by increasing knowledge, leading to increased ownership of bed-nets used by vulnerable households. Another study by Gertler and colleagues (2009) showed that there was a positive correlation between a household's consumption and measure of health in Indonesia.

Recently, MFIs in India have integrated their services into achieving better health care for poor households. Some MFIs, including the Microfinance Institutions Network (MFIN), run health camps by educating their clients about the basic health needs and management of diseases such as malaria, dengue, and HIV/AIDS. According to Metcalfe (2012), MFIs have achieved significant impact in areas such as neonatal and maternal mortality and infant and child feeding. Leatherman et al. (2011) look at the low marginal costs of MFIs as an indicator for them to participate and engage themselves in providing better health-care systems.

There is a contrasting perspective as well. Considering the Indian health situation, there could have been a strong linkage between microfinance and health care. Health-care providers need to look at the importance of the social intermediary role those MFIs play in local communities. However, the literature does not provide substantial insight on this aspect. Other impact studies show that there is no relationship between microfinance and health. For instance, the study by Desai and Tarozzi (2013) examined the effect of family planning services and microcredit in Ethiopia. They conducted baseline and follow-up surveys of a cross-section of households and found that none of the interventions significantly increased contraceptive use or the intent to use family planning methods over the control group. In 2004, Dohn and colleagues implemented and evaluated a thirteen-month health promotion programme targeting childhood illness and women's health in the Dominican Republic. They failed to show that microcredit led to an increase in health outcomes in all 11 of the indicators that they identified. Along similar lines, Smith, in his 2002 study about the comparison of conventional banking systems to that of the health bank model combining microfinance and health education services in urban slums of Ecuador, did not lead to an overall lower diarrhoea probability.

The recent literature fails to identify the reasons behind low health spending by poor households. Taking the example of India (which is a wide economy mixed with high social values, customs and traditions), the money, which borrowers get in the form of small loans, is running out into expenditures governed by social traditions and customs. According to Vijendra Rao (2001), poor households tend to spend heaps of money on celebrations to acquire social status and recognition in the society. He argues that publicly celebrated events serve two primary functions: they facilitate the maintenance of social reputations and networks of duty, and they act as venues for status-enhancing competitions. Further, the link between health and spending governed by social customs is not dealt with in existing literature. Hence, this chapter examines whether there is a correlation between microfinance and social spending based on the secondary and primary data collected.

According to Littlefield and colleagues (2003), one of the first things poor people all over the world do with new income from microenterprise is to invest in their children's education. There is an abundance of literature that focuses on the positive link between microfinance and attainment of education qualifications among the poorest households. Most of the recent literature focuses on whether or not microfinance led to a sizeable impact on education via literacy rates, number of years of schooling, school dropout rates, etc. In addition, the literature fails to identify any solid conclusion about the correlation between microfinance and education being positive.

One such impact evaluation looks at a microfinance programme in Uganda which showed that client households tend to spend more on schooling and education than do non-client households. Barnes and colleagues (2001), in their words, conclude, 'Clients have also been significantly more likely than non-clients to pay school charges for a non-household member.' On similar lines, Khandker (2001) found out that providing small loans to poor households led to a fall in dropout rates for children in the treatment group in comparison with non-treated households. Further, their study found that children stayed for a longer period at schools when their families received loans from MFIs. The Indian example of the Self-Employed Women's Association (SEWA) Bank, Gujarat, led to positive improvement in enrolment of boys in primary and secondary schooling in Ahmadabad. Over the period from 1997 to 1999, borrowing from the SEWA Bank had a positive impact on boys' secondary-school enrolment rates, raising them to 70%.

Holvoet (2004), in his study, looked at the specific effects of microfinance on childhood education. He looked at South India and gathered data on literacy rates and on how credit enters the household and who brings it in. The results were mixed. It did not matter who brought the credit in when it came in the form of direct bank–borrower credit delivery. However, in the cases where women got credit from women's associations, the money spent on childhood education somewhat increased in favour of girls' education but left the boys' education outcomes largely unchanged. Holvoet did not find any causal link or correlation between microloans and spending on children's education. In addition, he found that the gender of individual bank loan clients had not impacted their children's education. Hence, there is ambiguity in the data cited in the literature about linkages between education and microfinance.

Adding to this ambiguity, credit constraints often lead to negative impact on education in the context of poor households. For instance, Todd and Ralph (2007) looked at credit constraints and low incomes as the two reasons for the high number of school dropout rates. They took up panel data estimation to validate their results and concluded that while credit constraints were likely to influence the school dropout decisions of some students, the large majority of attrition of students from low-income families should be primarily attributed to reasons other than credit constraints.

Apart from credit constraints, literature exists on the quality of education where individuals face the choice between private schooling and public schooling. Considering India as an example, households living in rural areas are unable to afford the overwhelming costs of seeking good-quality education for their children. A study by Joanna Härmä (2009) analysed the effect of 'low-fee private' (LFP) schools on promoting education for all, taking the case of Uttar Pradesh in India. She based her study on a 13-village survey of 250 households and visits to 26 private and government schools in rural Uttar Pradesh, India. In particular, the paper explored the issue of whether private provision is affordable and accessible to poor rural parents. It found that LFP school costs were unaffordable for over half of the sampled children, including the majority of low-caste and Muslim families. It also found that while LFPs are greatly preferred under current conditions, what parents actually want is a well-functioning government school system.

Having discussed the recent literature on education, the question of how traditional values and customs govern the minds of the poor household's expenditure pattern remains a mystery that has to be solved. A poor household living in a rural area, when exposed to small loans, tends to spend on social functions to gain recognition in the society rather than spending on basic needs such as education. Thus, the available empirical evidence shows that households are spending on social occasions to develop social capital. By social capital, we mean the internal and social coherence of society, the norms and the values that govern interactions among people and the institutions in which they are embedded.

Nowadays, expenditure of households depends on a variety of issues and is specific when it comes to building social capital. Spending on social events to get recognized in society, an ambition to attain a high social status, is driving the households to spend on various cultural programmes, marriages, festivals, and other customary occasions. The growing literature suggests that the financial decision in the poor household is made mainly on social events, customs, culture, and traditions of the individuals who control income in the family. A study by Nazli Kibria (1998) looked at the women's garment industry in Bangladesh and the expenditure pattern of its members. Notwithstanding the historically limited economic autonomy of Bangladeshi women, their capacity to manage their money varied, with a significant proportion of female workers exercising complete control over their earnings. The socio-economic background influenced women's income control by determining the symbolic significance of their earnings and the capacity of male relatives to meet their conventional responsibilities towards women. Aside from a few young, unmarried employees, women's participation in the garment industry has not significantly threatened patriarchal family dynamics.

The literature has shown some plausible insights into social expenditure. For instance, the study by Cynthia Werner (1997) looked at consumption patterns in rural Kazakhstan with regard to changes in wedding feasts. The author points out that despite economic hardship post-Soviet transition to a market economy, rural Kazakhs have continued to spend a large amount of their income and resources on feasts and marriages. She found that exchanging gifts and utilizing imported goods led to the enhancement of social status and identity among rural Kazakhs. In her own words, she concluded that 'The process of further social stratification has intensified the level of competition in feasting and gift giving among the local elite. And the same process has generated resentment among poor households who find it more and more difficult to continue participating in the ritual economy.'

A recent study by Susan Wolcott (2013) studied the situation of rural credit markets in colonial India and how Indian cultivators spend on ceremonies, marriages, and funerals. She linked this leakage to the expense of increases in agricultural activity and investment. According to her, 'Indian cultivators spent a remarkable portion of their income on festivals, marriages and death ceremonies . . . For all of India, ceremonial expenditures for one year on average constituted 18 percent of annual crop values.' Further, she noted this tendency among poor households, who relatively spent more on ceremonies as compared to agricultural activities, and 'for those families, consumption clearly crowded out investment'. The reason for such high social expenditure is 'social caste' and how different castes demand the need for ceremonial expenditures. Further, the major implication of her study looked at how poor households took credit for funding ceremonies rather than investing in their agricultural business.

Some of the recent studies also throw some light on social exclusion as being the cause for spending on social events. The study by Bittman (2002) looked at social exclusion being a multidimensional concept explaining the significance of social identity, culture, agency, and power relations. His argument was that households spend on leisure activities due to social exclusion. He analysed the most recent household expenditure survey, which showed that consumption of leisure goods and services was powerfully determined by income. His conclusions looked at how low income can lead to exclusion from leisure participation.

Another study by Brown and colleagues (2007) looked at a panel estimation of rural villages in China on how there has been a sharp increase in socially observable spending. They suggested that 'social spending is either positional in nature (that is, motivated by status concern) or subject to herding behaviour'. They found that the welfare implications of spending in order to 'keep up with the traditions' are potentially large, particularly for poor households.

Practitioners of international development increasingly see microfinance as a viable strategy for reducing poverty and enhancing the economic independence of the world's poor. Microfinance schemes, group-based financing, poor people's access to financial resources, and the scheme's impact on different aspects of development and women's empowerment have all been the subject of research since its inception, and this research has been conducted in both rural and urban settings. The microfinance literature has begun to focus more on rural poor people. Increases in the financial inclusion of the poor have been a focus of anti-poverty and gender equality initiatives, with development resources being put to good use. According to the United Nations Capital Development Fund (2005), microfinance has helped to promote economic equality because of the close relationship between wealth and poverty. It is widely acknowledged that receiving a microloan can spur entrepreneurial spirit and give borrowers the means to better their own lives (Khaval 2010). By reducing poverty and giving women more economic independence, microfinance programmes can have a profound impact on entire neighbourhoods (Biswas 2014; Murthy et al. 2005). Microfinance initiatives let people get their hands on capital, allowing them to pursue careers in the unofficial economy (Kellett 2011; Mayoux 1999; Morduch 1999; Yunus 2003). Badatya (2006), Das and Jena (2012), and Onyuma and Shem (2005) all point to microfinance as a crucial method for reducing poverty and empowering women. Despite over 50 years of sustained effort, the traditional strategy in India has not delivered results in terms of financial inclusion, as noted by Renuka and Susan (Halan et al. 2011); in contrast, the microfinance industry has delivered remarkable results in a relatively short time.

3.3 The takeaways

A quick look at what others said in this chapter demonstrates that microfinance has evolved into a complex and multifaceted development tool. Far from being a uniform intervention, its outcomes vary across geographical contexts, institutional frameworks, and social settings. The studies collectively highlight both the achievements and the persistent shortcomings of microfinance as a means of poverty alleviation, livelihood generation, and women's empowerment.

3.3.1 Urban–rural dimensions of microfinance

One recurrent theme concerns the differential experiences of rural and urban borrowers. Bhimani (2021) illustrated that awareness levels of microfinance initiatives are similar in both urban and rural contexts, yet the rural poor report significantly higher levels of satisfaction with microfinance services. Rural borrowers also perceive greater improvements in income and social status, suggesting that microfinance may produce more tangible livelihood effects in less monetized economies. Complementing this, Gadekar's (2020) study of Pandharpur Taluka in Maharashtra emphasized the efficiency of private MFIs, which provide timely, doorstep credit without bureaucratic delay. However, his findings revealed that while financial services are accessible, the broader developmental needs of clients—such as training, technical assistance, and marketing—remain unmet. Similarly, Varghese (2020), in Gujarat, analysed diverse models including MFIs, joint-liability groups (JLGs), SEWA, farmer's clubs, and self-help groups (SHGs), underscoring that while each structure has certain strengths, systemic weaknesses such as high indebtedness, lack of trust, and overdependence on commercial banks undermine their long-term sustainability.

3.3.2 Microfinance and women's empowerment

Women's empowerment occupies a central place in microfinance discourse, yet the evidence is contested. Early studies such as Goetz and

Sen Gupta (1996) in Bangladesh reveal that while women are frequently the nominal borrowers, control over loan use is often exercised by men within households. This dynamic raises doubts about the depth of empowerment that microfinance can truly generate. Similarly, in Pakistan, Asim (2008) observed little measurable impact of microcredit on women's decision-making in areas such as health care, mobility, and child-rearing. By contrast, Pitt and Cartwright (2003) demonstrated that women's participation in microfinance in Bangladesh strengthens bargaining power within households, enhances independence in personal decisions, and expands opportunities for social mobility.

In India, a large body of work identifies more positive trajectories. Badatya (2006), studying SHGs in Andhra Pradesh, highlighted how group participation improves women's sense of self-worth, decision-making capacity, and solidarity. Panda (2009) similarly found that SHG-linked microfinance in Orissa, Jharkhand, and Chhattisgarh produces favourable outcomes in income, savings, and literacy, while Ranjula Bali Swain (2006) demonstrated that SHG households show greater economic resilience and improved self-confidence compared to control groups. Vachya and Kamaiah (2015) emphasized how SHG participation in Andhra Pradesh enhances women's ability to challenge traditional norms, including opposition to dowry and demands for property rights, while Chandani (2014) documented an increase in self-confidence, self-esteem, and social mobility among SHG participants in Chennai. Malleswari (2010) and Swapna (2017) highlighted the role of microfinance in promoting women's entrepreneurship, but both cautioned that financial inclusion must be paired with credit-plus services such as training, access to technology, and market support to be transformative.

Nevertheless, critical concerns persist. Sharma (2019), working in the slums of Delhi, demonstrated that up to 90% of SHG loans are diverted toward health-care expenditures rather than income-generating activities. While this improves women's physical and mental health, it raises concerns about sustainability and the long-term developmental potential of microfinance. Similarly, in Kerala, Sooryamoorthy (2005) argued that despite years of existence, many SHGs remain unable to leverage funds effectively for enterprise, pointing to structural weaknesses in their design and implementation. These findings highlight the tension between the aspirational objectives of microfinance and the practical realities of poor households facing urgent consumption needs.

3.3.3 Health, social capital, and collective action

Beyond direct financial outcomes, microfinance also contributes to health, social capital, and collective action. Sharma (2019) illustrated that SHG loans improve affordability of health care, reduce anxiety, and enhance household well-being. Rahman and Khan (2007), focusing on aquaculture projects in Bangladesh, demonstrated how women's participation in productive activities enhances their autonomy and agency. Sanyal (2009) provided an important sociological perspective, showing how access to microfinance in West Bengal strengthens women's social capital, collective action, and capacity to mobilize for community needs such as infrastructure, education, and sanitation. Such outcomes suggest that microfinance, when organized collectively, can extend empowerment from the private to the public sphere, challenging entrenched gender norms and opening new avenues for social reform.

3.3.4 Structural challenges and institutional critiques

Despite its potential, significant limitations persist. Dixon, Ritchie, and Siwale (2006) reported a wide gap between the high demand for microfinance and the limited reach of MFIs in Zambia. Musona (2004) documented inefficiencies in loan disbursement, which frustrate clients and reduce outreach, while Rathore (2017) noted that a large share of loans is used for non-income-generating activities despite being earmarked for enterprise. Labie and colleagues (2010) highlighted discriminatory practices in Uganda, where loan officers often exclude persons with disabilities due to biases and lack of accountability mechanisms.

The Andhra Pradesh microfinance crisis provides perhaps the most striking cautionary tale. As Shruti Saxena (2014) and subsequent observers noted, the rapid growth of MFIs, coupled with high interest rates, multiple lending, and coercive recovery practices, created a climate of over-indebtedness and borrower distress. The 2010 state ordinance regulating MFIs—through caps on interest rates, mandatory registration, and restrictions on multiple loans—precipitated a collapse in repayment rates from 99% to just 20% (Ghiyazuddin and Gupta 2012). This crisis damaged institutional legitimacy, drove clients back to moneylenders, and revealed the fragility of microfinance when market efficiency is prioritized over social responsibility.

3.3.5 Broader lessons and theoretical insights

The broader lessons from this literature are two-fold. First, as Barnes, Gaile, and Kimbombo (2001) and Bruton, Khavul, and Chavez (2011) argue, microfinance can indeed enhance income, asset ownership, and household well-being. However, as Karl (1995) and Mayoux (1999, 2009) emphasize, empowerment is a multidimensional process that requires more than financial access. It involves building technical skills, social capital, managerial capacity, and independence from patriarchal constraints. Mahanta and colleagues (2012) further warn that unless loans are paired with skill development, they may be diverted to consumption rather than investment. Institutional design also matters: Ledgerwood (1999) and Paxton and Fruman (1997) demonstrate that sustainability depends on balancing outreach with financial viability, with savings-led models showing greater resilience than credit-led approaches.

3.4 Thematic considerations and key takeaways

3.4.1 Microfinance and poverty alleviation

- Positive findings: many studies (Gadekar 2020; World Bank and Badatya 2006) show that MFIs help reduce poverty by increasing access to credit, improving household assets, and generating income.
- Limitations: concerns remain about debt burden, targeting of the 'core poor', and overdependence on loans rather than sustainable income (Leatherman and Dunford 2010; Varghese 2020).
- Gap: poverty reduction is not uniform—social obligations and non-productive expenditures dilute the developmental potential of loans.

3.4.2 Microfinance and health

- Positive impacts: MFIs integrating health services show improvements in awareness and outcomes (Dunford 2001 on HIV/AIDS; Metcalfe 2012 on neonatal/maternal health; Pronyk et al. 2006 on domestic abuse reduction).
- Contradictory evidence: other studies (Desai and Tarozzi 2013; Dohn 2004; Smith 2002) found no significant improvement in health outcomes despite access to microcredit.
- Underlying issue: a large share of microloans is spent on social obligations and customs instead of health care, limiting direct health impact.
- Gap: there is a lack of research on the link between social spending and health neglect.

3.4.3 Microfinance and education

- Positive evidence: studies in Uganda and India (SEWA Bank and Khandker 2001) show reduced dropout rates and improved enrolment.
- Mixed results: Holvoet (2004) found gendered effects—women's credit slightly boosted girls' education but had little impact on that of boys.
- Negative trends: credit constraints and costs of private schooling reduce benefits (Härmä 2009); Todd and Ralph 2007).
- Gap: there is no clear consensus on whether microfinance directly enhances education since loans are often diverted to non-educational expenses.

3.4.4 Microfinance and social traditions/cultural spending

- Strong theme: numerous studies (Rao and Woolcock 2013; Werner et al. 2007) highlight that poor households spend heavily on weddings, funerals, festivals, and rituals to maintain social status and networks.

- Effects: this 'status spending' often crowds out investment in productive activities such as farming or business.
- Regional variations:
  - o India: ceremonial expenditures take up ~18% of annual crop values (Wolcott 2013);
  - o Kazakhstan: feasting and gift-giving escalate competition and social inequality (Werner et al. 2007);
  - o China: increased positional spending is driven by status concerns (Brown et al. 2011).
- Gap: there is insufficient exploration of how microfinance indirectly sustains social inequality through cultural expenditure.

3.4.5 Microfinance and women's empowerment

- Positive outcomes: many studies show that microfinance enhances women's agency, decision-making, mobility, and social capital (Pitt and Khandker 2003; Sanyal 2009; Swain 2006).
- Limitations: empowerment is often constrained by patriarchal norms—loans are sometimes controlled by men or diverted to household/social obligations (Asim 2008; Goetz and Gupta 1996).
- Diversity in findings: some contexts show significant improvements (SEWA, SHGs in Andhra Pradesh), while others find minimal or no empowerment (Das 2011 in Assam).
- Gap: there has been little analysis of the trade-off between empowerment through credit and the burden of repayment/social obligations.

3.4.6 MFIs: Models, challenges, and performance

- Different models: SHGs, JLGs, SEWA, farmer's clubs, and MFI profit models each have strengths and weaknesses (Varghese 2020).
- Challenges:
  - o there is low awareness and trust in rural areas,
  - o there is heavy reliance on external funds (Varghese 2020),
  - o there are delayed disbursements (Musona 2004),

  - o there is weak savings mobilization (Musona and Coetzee 2001; Tamrat 2016).
- Mixed client satisfaction: some borrowers are satisfied with services and empowerment (Rathore 2017), but many still seek informal loans for flexibility.
- Gap: there is a need for non-financial services (training, health education, business skills) to complement credit.

3.4.7 Cross-cutting insights

- Divergent outcomes: microfinance works better when combined with non-financial interventions (health, education, training).
- Cultural dimension: social traditions and status-driven expenditures significantly weaken the intended poverty alleviation and development goals.
- Gendered experience: women often benefit, but empowerment depends heavily on local cultural norms and household power dynamics.
- Research gaps:
  - o there is limited focus on social spending as a determinant of loan effectiveness,
  - o there is a lack of causal evidence connecting microfinance to sustained improvements in health/education,
  - o there is insufficient evaluation of the long-term sustainability of MFIs under different models.

The dynamics governing the borrowing behaviour of microcredit borrowers show the trends of growing social capital as a motive to drain expenditure on social occasions; additionally, social stigma in Indian societies also plays an important role. Poverty reduction among poor households means not only development of health care services, better educational facilities or setting up a new business but also expanding human capabilities by avoiding violence. A recent study in Kerala looked at the impact of marital violence on the economic outcomes of women in rural households. Many studies have looked at the correlation between marital violence and economic prosperity but have often neglected the link through credit constraints. In achieving social status and sticking to the social norms of the society, households are pouring money into celebrating festivals and occasions rather than spending on essential economic needs.

Adding to the above reason of social violence, Chen (2011) looked at the social link, peer effect, and status concern as being the motivation behind high gift expenditure in China. He tried to answer the question raised by Banerjee and Duflo (2011), 'Why do poor people spend more on social occasions such as marriages, festivals and other ceremonies?' According to his evaluation, he found that 'a 1% increase in peers' gift spending per occasion leads to a .13–.34% increase in one's own gift per occasion'. Chen (2011) explained that it is easier for poor households to climb the social ladder while engaging themselves with the rich rather than insuring themselves against the future risk (risk pooling strategy): 'Overall, large social spending may result in negative externalities and welfare loss, especially for households living close to subsistence'—but this is subject to Chen's findings on gift expenditure as compared to risk-pooling mechanisms.

However, no literature has seriously and strongly looked into the link between microfinance and social expenditure (spending on weddings, funerals, festivals, etc.). Anthropologists and sociologists did look at the trend on social expenditure, which is being imposed upon through social pressure, but economists are still in the early stages of finding a causal link between access to credit and that credit being used to finance social occasions. What an economist would think is that it was individuals' own satisfaction or behaviour that makes them spend on social events, but sociologists argue that being under pressure, poor people focus on social spending and neglect valuable spending on health outcomes and educational outcomes. The above papers do provide an insight into growing social expenditure, but this is not economics. Hence, more research on economic evidence has to be performed to look at the causal link. Hence, this work tries to attempt to fill the gap by looking at the impact of microcredit on festivals and other social expenditures varying across households, limiting its conclusions to the data collected and analysed.

The Andhra Pradesh crisis in microfinance is another dimension, which prompted the state government to implement stringent regulations on the operations of MFIs in undivided Andhra Pradesh.

Shruti Saxena (2014) from the University of Minnesota published a paper after studying the microfinance crisis in Andhra Pradesh. Her findings can be summarized as follows.

In 2006, the initial indications of difficulties in microfinance in Andhra Pradesh emerged. Referred to as the 'Krishna crisis' due to its occurrence in Krishna district, this event transpired when the state government closed 50 branches of two major MFIs—Share and Spandana. The government asserted that these organizations imposed exorbitant interest rates on clients, employed abusive recovery practices, and appropriated clients from the government-sponsored SHG programme, citing these as justifications for their closure. The shutdown adversely affected lending and recovery cycles, yet its impact was minimal and was resolved promptly. Nonetheless, the private MFIs experienced a shock and united to enhance their bargaining power, once more pledging to adopt voluntary regulation. Sa-Dhan, an industry association for MFIs established in 1999, advocated for the formulation of a voluntary code of conduct in response to the Krishna crisis. The MFIs adopted this code and committed to lowering interest rates. In 2009, the MFIN was founded for non-banking financial company–MFIs (NBFC–MFIs). External observers of the industry perceived Sa-Dhan as ineffective, and its efficacy was called into question following a series of crises. MFIN announced that its members would advocate for responsible lending and adhere to a code of conduct.

Prior to the onset of difficulties, the 2000s had been a prosperous period for microfinance in India. Vikram Akula (2010), founder of SKS Microfinance, experienced significant prominence as the representative of microfinance. SKS Microfinance was the inaugural entity to access the Indian capital market via an initial public offering (IPO) in July 2010. This development is noteworthy given that SKS Microfinance initially operated as a non-profit organization and was not anticipated to pursue an IPO. The offering was oversubscribed, resulting in a swift increase in share prices. These were perceived as indicators of the profitability of financing the impoverished, suggesting that the golden age of microfinance had commenced.

However, not all individuals concurred with this perspective. Dissenters emphasized the market's bubble-like expansion (Rozas and Sinha 2010). Critics have also highlighted saturation and potential oversupply in the microcredit market in Andhra Pradesh. The oversupply is thought to have resulted from client poaching by organizations aiming to achieve their targets and from multiple lending to consumers, leading to individuals managing loans from several MFIs simultaneously.

Allegations of abusive practices by intermediary agents of private MFIs emerged in the vernacular press before gaining attention in the national media. Suicides in Andhra Pradesh are frequently influenced by agricultural trends and are regrettably prevalent. In this instance, over 70 suicides were purportedly associated with individuals' inability to repay MFIs (Biswas 2010). The state government referenced these suicides as justification for intervening to safeguard citizens from the unethical practices of private MFIs. The Andhra Pradesh Microfinance Institutions (Regulation of Money Lending) Ordinance 2010 was enacted on 15 October 2010 to mitigate oversupply and coercive recovery practices.

Immediate mandates included the requirement for all MFIs to register with the government, delineate their operational areas, disclose interest rates charged, and specify the systems employed for operations and recovery. In the absence of this, they could no longer execute operations. Sanctions were delineated for entities employing coercive recovery methods. Organizations were prohibited from granting multiple loans to a single borrower, and a cap was established on the total interest charged.

Following the enactment of the ordinance, lending and recovery ceased entirely. Politicians urged individuals to refrain from repaying the MFIs. This resulted in two significant consequences: it negatively impacted collections for MFIs (collection rates for organizations in Andhra Pradesh declined from 99% to 20% (Ghiyazuddin and Gupta 2012); and clients who failed to repay their loans became ineligible for subsequent loans. The liquidity of the MFIs diminished significantly due to restricted interest rates and discouragement of repayment by state officials. Commercial banks ceased extending credit due to apprehensions regarding potential losses.

At this juncture, it is essential to elucidate the term 'crisis', which has been frequently employed in reference to microfinance in Andhra Pradesh and, subsequently, in India. This constituted a crisis for multiple reasons. First, multiple individuals committed suicide due to their inability to repay debts. Although blame-shifting has been prevalent, MFIs contributed to individuals' desperation by prioritizing market efficiency over the original pro-poor vision of microfinance. Second, this ordinance diminished confidence in MFIs and prompted commercial banks to reassess their exposure. Although the scrutiny may have been justified, an abrupt shock in a financial market induces additional fragility. This ordinance diminished the legitimacy of MFIs in the perception of their clients and investors. Third, the state government may have provided short-term assistance to citizens but ultimately jeopardized their long-term interests by rendering them non-viable clients. This reduction in access to financial resources compelled numerous individuals to revert to moneylenders. This served as a catalyst for the Reserve Bank of India to formulate essential regulatory and policy reforms.

3.5 Conclusion

In conclusion, the other studies portray microfinance not as a panacea but as a conditional and context-dependent instrument. It has enabled millions of poor households to access credit, accumulate assets, and, in many cases, enhance women's agency. Yet, it has also been misapplied for short-term consumption, undermined by institutional weaknesses, and tarnished by exploitative practices (See Box 3.1).

Box 3.1 NABARD studies on impact of microfinance

A. NABCONS Study on Micro Enterprise Development Programme (MEDP)s in Rajasthan

An Impact Assessment Study of three Micro Enterprise Development Programmes (MEDPs) was conducted by Rajasthan Regional Office through NABARD Consultancy Services (NABCONS). Of the three MEDPs selected, two were on Applique and Embroidery both in Barmer district and one on Papad & Badi making in Banswara district. The objective of the study was to assess the impact of the programme on the beneficiaries and also identify the problems faced by the beneficiaries and offer suggestions on the same.

A sample of 10 beneficiaries across all the three programmes were selected for the study. All of the three MEDPs were conducted during the FYs 2020-21 and 2021-22. The major observations of the study were:

1. Most of the beneficiaries were involved in job work and had not set up independent enterprises.
2. Size of businesses set up was very small. As a result, beneficiaries were unable to realize economies of scale.
3. Lack of marketing arrangements was one of the reasons affecting the profitability of microenterprises. It was felt that proper market link-ups post MEDP training is to be provided by institutions concerned.

B. Studies conducted by Centre for Research on Financial Inclusion and Microfinance (CrFim)

NABARD provides budgetary support to the Centre for Research on Financial Inclusion and Microfinance (CRFIM) set up at Bankers Institute of Rural Development (BIRD), Lucknow for conducting research, publication of 'Journal on Microfinance Research' & 'Trend Reports on Financial Inclusion' and organizing national level seminars. Findings of two studies taken up during FY 2022-23 are given in the following paragraphs.

1. *'Analysing Micro Enterprises financed by Public Sector Banks (with SHG Linkages), SFBs and MFIs*

The study was conducted across 8 districts in 4 states, viz., Uttar Pradesh, Tamil Nadu, Karnataka and Maharashtra and covered 192 stakeholders comprising of 144 microenterprises and 48 branches of PSBs, MFIs and SFBs. The primary objectives of the study were to (i) highlight the key characteristics of the microenterprise sector (ii) assess the demand for and the flow of credit into the sector; and (iii) evaluate the consequent gap in financing the credit needs of the sample microenterprises.

Major Findings

(i) Lending to the sample microenterprises are done mostly in the group-based model to women by financing institutions. The average age of sample clients is approximately 40 years having sound financial literacy.
(ii) Majority of the microenterprises are engaged in retail or trading activities followed by manufacturing sector.
(iii) Multiple memberships in formal institutions were observed due to non-availability of sufficient funds, non-availability of loan when needed and difficulty in getting second/third loan cycle.
(iv) The total credit supply to sample microenterprises by MFIs is 37.5% of the overall debt supply followed by SFBs.
(v) Taking loan from MFIs is preferred due to speed, lesser documentation work, collateral free nature of loan and flexible repayment schedules.
(vi) The rate of interest charged by SFBs was considerably higher than MFIs and PSBs.
(vii) Major challenges faced by financing institutions in microcredit were risks in lending, documentation, loan recovery, higher operational cost, and multiple lending.

One Decade of MFI Crisis : Revisiting Rural Credit Market in Andhra Pradesh and Telangana

The study was jointly conducted by CRFIM and LEAD at Krea University (IFMR LEAD). The study covered 347 women SHG members in AP and Telangana. The study focused on (i) diagnosing the causes of the massive debt bubble in AP, (ii) impact of rural credit market following the MFI crisis, (iii) growth of SHG credit linkage & microfinance in AP, and (iv) best practices in MFIs in the post MFI crisis period.

Major Findings

(i) Post-crisis, SHGs have emerged as the major source of borrowing with 91% of respondents having borrowed only from SHGs.

(ii) In the absence of MFIs, SHG loans from the SRMFI Sand banks were the alternative sources of credit among the sample SHG borrowers.

Due to the saturation of SHG-BLP in both states, the growth of savings-linked SHGs has decreased. However, the growth of savings outstanding increased notably in the states (31.60%) as compared to the national average of 13.10%, indicating peoples' trust and faith in the SHG eco-system, post MFI crisis.

4
The Methodological Approach

4.1 Introduction

This chapter delineates the comprehensive process of data collection, refinement, analysis, and interpretation from the chosen two geographical locations in India. The borrower's perspective has been collected and examined to comprehend the comprehensive overview of microcredit utility in the state of Telangana. The comprehensive literature review informed the research objectives and assumption concerning the efficacy of microcredit and its conceptual framework.

This work combined qualitative and quantitative approaches to assess clients' utilization and repayment of microcredit. It used a quantitative approach, having a descriptive purpose. Kothari (2004) stated that descriptive research can explain what is happening; it has no control over variables. The qualitative technique is used to enhance the quantitative approach (Gabrielian 1999) since it facilitates the evaluation of respondents' perspectives through personal intuition (Kothari 2004). The study predominantly utilized primary data sources.

The microcredit study focused on borrowers from a designated bank branch of a public-sector bank and a microfinance institution (MFI) established by the Government of Telangana, operating inside Telangana. One hundred completed questionnaires were acquired through the author's personal visits, emails, and telephone discussions. The self-administered structured questionnaire consisted of forty-seven items concerning age, education, amount of microcredit obtained, activity, usefulness for the specified activity, and diversion for other social and customary needs. Out of the total 47 questions, 24 assessed the demographics and social and economic situations of the borrowers, whereas 23 analysed the microcredit obtained and its application for both intended and unintentional objectives. The information collected from this

Microcredit Misallocation? P. Gargi Rao, Oxford University Press. © P. Gargi Rao 2026.
DOI: 10.1093/9780197910573.003.0004

questionnaire was intended to enable both qualitative and quantitative analysis. The demographic characteristics of the respondents have been examined by descriptive statistics and cross-tabulation. The financial performance indicators have been developed following the compilation and analysis of the acquired data. The main aim of this data collection was to study participants' loan utilization behaviour and evaluate its link with their socio-economic status, loan amount, company needs, and societal requirements. The data enabled the correlation between the loan amount obtained from the lending institution and the sustainability criteria of the borrower/participant. Interviews with participants indicated that upon obtaining a loan for a microbusiness, they anticipated being able to invest the funds; yield returns; repay the bank loan from these returns; provide for their families; and meet social, religious, and customary obligations. Chapter 5 elaborates on the approaches adopted to collect and analyse the data. The poll included microcredit borrowers associated with two prominent banks and the state government's microfinance facility.

A total of 100 (50 + 50) filled-in questionnaires were obtained from participants via home visits, interviews at bank-organized meetings, and data gained from bank managers. The questionnaire consisted of 47 enquiries concerning age, education, amount of microcredit obtained, activity, usefulness for the specified activity, and diversion for other social and customary needs. Out of the 47 questions, 24 assessed the borrowers' demographics, social, and economic characteristics, while 23 investigated the microcredit obtained and its utilization for both planned and unintentional objectives. The study delineates participant perception attributes, including the inadequacy of the loan for the intended enterprise, prioritization of personal obligations and social needs over business investment, improved financial literacy among female beneficiaries post-engagement with the loan product, opportunities for socialization enabled by temporary financial capacity, and familial responsibilities. The survey indicates that certain people have obtained microcredit from various sources, including a consumption loan alongside a business loan. The subsequent sections offer an overview of the borrower survey research instruments, the data collection methods, and the proposed integrated model formulated by the author.

4.2 Objectives and assumptions of the study

4.2.1 Objectives

Literature on microfinance has elucidated the industry's benefits and challenges in detail. It has facilitated the identification of relevant research gaps and established the specific objectives for the current study. This led us to assess the unintended utilization of microcredit by borrowers, identify both credit and non-credit financial requirements of microcredit borrowers, derive policy implications, and propose corrective actions for the identified deficiencies and shortcomings in the microcredit system. Therefore, the study was founded on these objectives:

a) to assess the influence of microcredit on the poverty levels of borrowers and its utility for the purpose other than it is intended to,
b) to assess the influence of microcredit on borrowers' perceptions of MFIs in India,
c) to draw policy conclusions and propose a way forward to achieve the objectives of microcredit.

4.2.2 Assumption

The conceptual benefits of microcredit include investing small amounts in microenterprises and minor businesses; generating income from these investments; repaying the loan with interest; fulfilling family consumption needs—which encompass expenditures on food, clothing, education, health, funerals, marriages, births, travel, entertainment, and social and religious obligations—and reinvesting the remaining funds into the business to sustain economic activity. Microcredit is not provided to directly address the socio-economic requirements of the borrower, such as expenditure on food, clothing, education, health care, funerals, weddings, childbirth, travel, entertainment, and social or religious obligations.

An assumption is established to address the research questions and fulfil the study's objectives. This study formulated assumptions regarding the utility of microcredit, the intended benefits of microcredit, and the borrower perception attributes that affect the concept of microcredit.

Informed by the literature review and research objectives, the following assumptions are established to ascertain the unintended utility of microcredit by borrowers, derive policy implications, and propose solutions to rectify deficiencies in borrower identification and the amount of microcredit disbursed:

- Assumption 1: microcredit is not utilized by the borrowers for the intended purpose but diverted to the unintended purpose by the borrowers.
- Assumption 2: there is no policy in India to address the financial requirements of the borrowers to meet their social, religious, cultural, consumption, and customary needs.
- Assumption 3: the microcredit offered by the institutions is not adequate either to meet the business needs or to meet the social needs.

4.3 Study design

The study design serves as the framework for executing the current book-writing project. An appropriate study design selected in accordance with the study's objectives will guarantee the research's effectiveness and efficiency. A conclusive descriptive research methodology employing a quantitative approach has been adopted to ascertain the unintended objectives of microcredit, the adequacy perceptions of borrowers, and the policy measures necessary to align microcredit with its intended purposes, specifically addressing the financial needs related to social, customary, consumption, religious, and cultural activities of borrowers. Conclusive research is a structured and definitive study conducted to test pre-specified assumptions and analyse the relationships among variables. The sample size in conclusive research is typically adequate and representative of the population, with data analysis being quantitative. The author has conducted descriptive research, a subcategory of conclusive research. Descriptive analysis is primarily utilized in social science and economic research contexts where the author lacks direct control over the study variables. All indicators are assessed regardless of their controllability and reported as they are. The research design employed in this study utilizes a quantitative inferential control methodology. The methodology is quantitative as the research processes entail the production of substantial data, which underwent meticulous quantitative analysis in an organized fashion. The research methodology is classified as inferential as it employs rigorous quantitative analysis to deduce characteristics of the broader population (Kothari and Garg 2014).

4.3.1 Study model

Based on the examined microfinance theories, research methods, domains, and methodologies in the extensive literature, two conceptual frameworks have been developed for lender perception and borrower behaviour for further analysis (Figs 4.1 and 4.2).

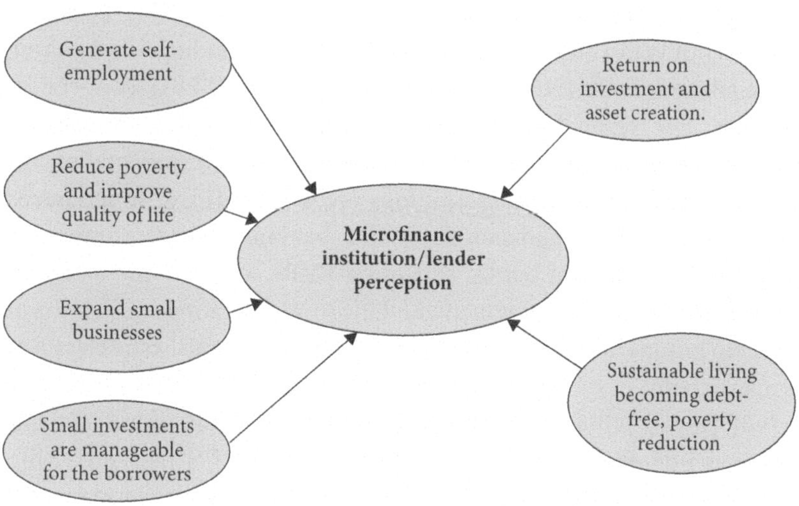

Fig. 4.1 Conceptual framework for MFI/lender perception of the financial performance of microcredit in India
Source: Prepared by the author.

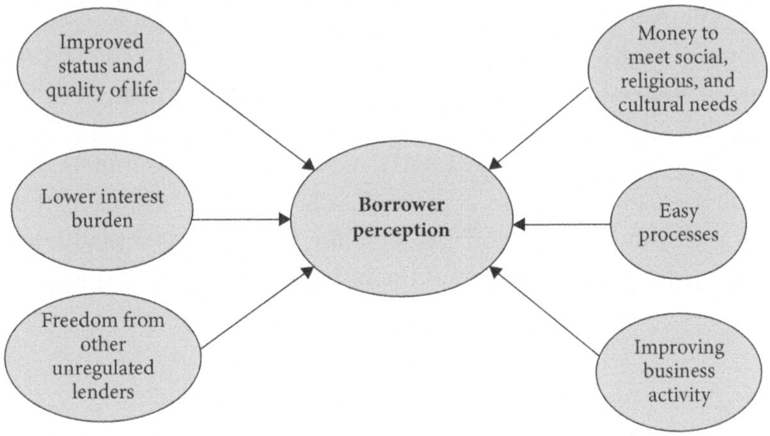

Fig. 4.2 Conceptual framework for borrower perception of microcredit
Source: Designed by the author.

4.3.2 Target population

'Microfinance' is an all-encompassing term. This encompasses microcredit and micro-savings. The credit encompasses lending activities. Micro-lending institutions are classified as MFIs, including non-banking financial companies (NBFCs), small finance banks (SFBs), cooperative societies, and regional rural banks (RRBs). To date, no comprehensive list of all categories of MFI has been issued by any governmental organization. The Microfinance Institutions Network (MFIN) functions as the self-regulatory organization for non-banking finance companies. Scheduled commercial banks, excluding RRBs, also provide loans for micro activities, self-employment, and income-generating endeavours of self-help groups and small enterprises. These loans can also be classified as microcredit.

NBFCs and MFIs are governed by the Reserve Bank of India (RBI). Consequently, this work focuses on the NBFC–MFIs registered with the RBI for which a complete sample frame is accessible. Consequently, the RBI's enumeration of NBFC–MFIs as of 30 June 2018, comprising 86 NBFC–MFIs situated in prominent Indian cities, constituted the focal population for the author. Few studies have primarily concentrated on the aforementioned institutions to comprehend their perception of financial performance. The institution list is nearly representative of the entire country as it encompasses all major cities.

To analyse the borrower perspective, one public-sector bank in Hyderabad and a state-run MFI serving borrowers from an urban fringe have been selected. The borrowers of the target institutions were primarily located on the peripheries of the Hyderabad and Badangpet municipal corporations. Several borrowers relocated from various regions of the country to Hyderabad and its surrounding areas in pursuit of employment opportunities. Consequently, the selected borrowers can be considered nearly emblematic of the entire population. The primary data collection spanned approximately six months, from January 2022 to July 2022.

4.3.3 Sample design

A sample design functions as a framework or blueprint for the selection of survey samples from a defined population of interest. A mixed sampling methodology, integrating both probability and non-probability sampling, was employed in the sample design. A direct random probability sampling technique was utilized to evaluate lenders' perceptions of loan performance indicators affecting borrowers' economic conditions. Every MFI within the designated sample frame possessed an equal probability of being included in the sample. It allowed the author to infer conclusions regarding the target populations from which the sample was obtained.

The non-probability convenience sampling technique was employed to analyse the borrower attributes influencing the perception of microcredit. The borrowers of the MFIs are geographically diverse. A comprehensive list of details regarding the borrowers of the MFIs was not readily accessible. Consequently, the borrowers were contacted via the MFIs with which they are presently affiliated. Borrowers were primarily situated within 100 kilometres of Hyderabad's outskirts.

Accordingly, the specified institutions were approached and requested to provide information on their branch offices where regular meetings for borrowers took place. Meetings involved direct engagement with the borrowers alongside data gathered through surveys from them. Convenience sampling was employed to investigate borrowers' impressions of one or more microfinance organizations due to the institutions' privacy and disclosure concerns, along with the authors' time and expense constraints. No research has been found that investigates borrower attitudes of the urban slums in Hyderabad. Thus, the borrowers from Hyderabad MFIs were chosen for the present study.

4.3.4 Sample size

The sample size was determined after thorough discussions and interviews with the lending managers of the banks. The geographical region for the sample was determined based on the density of institutional loan activity; thereafter, the availability and accessibility of beneficiaries was considered. A random selection of 25% of borrowers from a defined geographical region was designated as a sample reflecting the beneficiary community.

The questionnaires were disseminated at two sites: one at the borrowers' activity site and two at the MFIs' location. The respondents who filled out questionnaires at the MFI primarily comprised persons who attended the MFI to make instalment payments and to seek extensions for overdue sums.

A questionnaire consisting of 20 questions was developed for the lender perception survey and sent to the institution's managers, who coordinated with their field and other personnel to complete it. Before distributing the questionnaires, conversations were held with the branch manager to reduce bias and influence. The branch manager disseminated the questionnaire to all relevant personnel, gathered the completed replies, standardized the language and clarity of the answers, and returned the surveys.

As a general guideline, a minimum sample size of 100 is required for result validation. This study examined the sole MFI operated by the state government of Telangana as well as the largest public-sector commercial bank in the region. Both institutions agreed to extend their support for the research endeavour. Meetings were arranged with the branch officers, and the author accompanied them to the loan meetings with their borrowers. In accordance with the aforementioned route, 100 questionnaires

(50 from each group) were completed by the borrowers of the affiliated MFIs. All 100 completed questionnaires were retained as none were deemed unsuitable due to the author's physical presence during the data collection process.

4.3.5 Sampling procedure

The method utilized for the primary data collection of the questionnaires was focused on the perceptions of lenders and borrowers. Three approaches were utilized for the lender questionnaires: in-person visits, telephone interviews, and sending the questionnaire to randomly selected financial institutions. The lender questionnaire was meticulously designed in Excel for distribution to the specified email address and to be immediately filled out by the appropriate individual inside the institutions. The personnel website of each institution was scrutinized to ascertain the suitable contact (chiefly the branch manager) capable of completing the questionnaire via telephone. Performance evaluation reports, progress reports, and yearly returns were collected and evaluated from the institutions' websites. In Hyderabad, numerous staff visits were undertaken to gather completed questionnaires from each institution, with the objective of improving the response rate and clarifying potential biases in the responses as well as ways to address them.

All questionnaires on the borrower side were finalized through in-person visits with the borrowers at two designated institutions in Hyderabad. The entities were the rural branch of a public-sector bank branch and the state-run microfinance institution (SRMFI), Government of Telangana, Hyderabad, functioning in Balapur village of Badangpet municipality.

The SRMFI was the first MFI that allowed us to visit its borrowers. The meeting was arranged and organized by officials. The author selected Balapur as the location for the borrowers and communicated this to the regional manager. The SRMFI is a Telangana government organization dedicated to the economic empowerment of women. This was specifically chosen to examine the economic behaviour of women in poverty and microenterprises. Fifty completed questionnaires were successfully obtained from the borrowers of the SRMFI. The rural branch of a public-sector bank, Vanasthalipuram branch, was the second institution to extend data support. A significant number of their borrowers were dispersed, allowing for an extensive analysis of the economic behaviour of small borrowers. Consequently, upon obtaining the necessary authorization and coordination from the branch office personnel, the borrowers were contacted and asked to complete the questionnaire. During the primary data collection process, 50 completed questionnaires were obtained from Punjab National Bank (PNB) borrowers. The sample size of 100 completed questionnaires satisfied the minimum requirement, prompting the author to advance with data analysis and the compilation of the research work.

4.4 Questionnaire design

The lender perception research questionnaire comprised 20 interrelated questions requiring direct responses. The responses had to be meticulously considered; otherwise, the initial answer may have conflict with the subsequent one. The initial section of the questionnaire gathered fundamental data regarding the respondents. The questionnaire was not intentionally structured into distinct sections and thus lacked compartmentalization. The questions flowed easily, appearing to overlap: this was intentional. A comprehensive assessment of the respondents was conducted through the application of descriptive statistics and cross-tabulation.

The identical statistical tools, specifically descriptive statistics and cross-tabulations, were utilized to assess the institution-related information in the questionnaire. The lender's perception was employed to correlate the lender's viewpoint with the borrower's perspective and the actual circumstances following the credit extended by the lender and utilized by the borrower. The assumption posited that the borrowers were employing the credit for unintended purposes of microcredit. The lender's perception delineated the intended purpose of microcredit. Table 4.1 presents a detailed description of the sections, variables, and items included in the lender perception questionnaire.

The borrower's questionnaire was created to collect the demographic information of the borrower and their behaviour, which included name,

Table 4.1 Lender perception of loans and borrowers' economic and social status

Constructs	Measurement items
Activities of the lender	Banking and activities of microfinance—micro-saving and microcredit (micro-investment)
Willingness to lend to the poorest of the poor	Ability to lend to the poorest of the poor
Regularity in lending to microbusiness activities	Spread of micro lending across various microbusiness activities
Limitations in lending to microbusinesses	Sufficiency of limits
Loans not secured	Impact of unsecured loans on repayment
Intentions of the loan are clear to the lender, and accordingly, the loans are given	Percentage of loans used for the intended purpose
The lender knows to identify the prospective borrower	To what extent is the lender's knowledge put into use to identify the borrower?
The lender is aware of the behaviour of the borrower to invest the borrowed money in the intended activity	Factual situation in relation to the lender's awareness
Lender's awareness of the percentage of utilization	Actual percentage of utilization
Action against the recalcitrant borrower available	Impact of the action if taken—null if not taken or consequences of non-taking of action
Unable to repay the loan	Extent of inability to repay the loan
Change in the quality of life of the borrower should be visible	Extent of change in the quality of life of the borrower
Awareness of the lender about the microcredit intervention to poverty reduction	Level of understanding of the lender about the microcredit intervention
Lenders can suggest remedial measures in the microcredit policy	Width of policy recommendations
Consumption loans available to the borrowers	Impact of consumption loans on borrowers/business activities
Annual targets should be available	Extent of targets
The law enforcement mechanism is the tool to recover the loan	Extent of use of law enforcement by the lender
Second-time loans are available for the borrowers with acceptable repayment behaviour	Extent of utility of the facility

Source: Prepared by the author.

age, gender, education, marital status, number of children, household income, and additional socio-economic data; credit-related information, including loan amount, outstanding loan balance, and intended purpose as perceived by the lender; and utility data reflecting the social commitments for which the loan was utilized, encompassing marriages, fares, festivals, education, funerals, religious activities, gifts, pilgrimages, repayment of other debts, and other social obligations.

The identical statistical tools and techniques previously utilized for lender perception nominal scale items—specifically descriptive frequencies and cross-tabulations—were employed for the borrower behaviour-based research questionnaire. A total of 48 questions were presented, comprising endogenous and exogenous parameters categorized into 3 groups: 1—demographic variable, 2—loan purpose variable, and 3—loan utility behaviour variable. The endogenous latent constructs assessed borrowers' perceptions of microcredit via three observable statements. The exogenous latent constructs that directly influence borrower perception encompassed the opportunity to fulfil social needs through the diversion of the loan (unintended purpose), the enhancement of women's status within the household resulting from the loan's unified application, and the augmentation of financial knowledge. All exogenous latent constructs were assessed via observable variables, with the exception of borrower satisfaction, which was evaluated through observable statements regarding their credit. All attributes of borrower behaviour were quantified using numerical values and percentages.

4.5 The technique employed for analysis of data collected

The problem statement outlines the misallocation of loans by the impoverished for unintended purposes. While poverty alleviation is the primary objective of microcredit, the impoverished borrowers prioritize social obligations over financial investments; profit generation; debt repayment with interest; family consumption; and adherence to social, religious, and cultural commitments. Randomized control trials (RCTs), which necessitate a control group and a treatment group, involve waiting for a designated period to observe the investment and consumption behaviour of borrowers. However, such an approach was not intended for this work due to its considerable time and energy demands. It would be unethical for the author to have extend loans to one group while withholding them from another group and subsequently assessing their behaviour for research purposes. The RCT approach in both groups advocates for the assessment of individuals with comparable socio-economic conditions. Consequently, RCT is not utilized in this study.

The identification of dependent and independent variables, the derivation of regressions, and the analysis of data using statistical and econometric tools are infeasible when the spending behaviour of the impoverished is influenced more by their customs, beliefs, practices, sentiments, and immediate needs than by business and investment considerations. The primary objective was to provide evidence that the intended purpose of microcredit is not fulfilled. Consequently, the author employed graphs, percentages, and tables to convey the findings. The study examined the loans acquired and utilized by borrowers in small denominations from two institutions: the rural branch of a public-sector bank and the SRMFI of the Government of Telangana.

The data was analysed and presented in tables, percentages, and various types of charts for the reader's ease of comprehension. Consideration has been given to ensuring that both the technical reader and the average individual can readily discern the challenges and opportunities associated with the utilization of microcredit by borrowers. Policymakers and bankers lacking professional training in economics are anticipated to value results expressed in percentage terms better than those explained through other econometric models and regression analyses. Consequently, the author has employed tables, percentages, and charts to elucidate the misallocation of loans by borrowers towards unintended purposes and social expenditures rather than investing in designated business activities.

For the collection of data, two institutions lending to microbusinesses were randomly selected based on the accessibility convenience of the author.

As explained in Annexure IV, the borrowers' behaviour and perception are the foundation of this work, and the questions therein lead to testing the assumption. The borrowers of the rural branch of a public-sector bank included 32 female borrowers and 18 male borrowers, whereas the data collected from the SRMFI microfinance facility of the Government of Telangana were fully from 50 female borrowers. The data collected comprises the following:

A. The money required for running the family of the borrower
   - Household income of the borrower
   - Microcredit taken from the MFI
   - Microcredit due to be repaid to MFI
   - Microcredit utilized for microbusiness (the intended purpose)
   - Microcredit utilized for unintended purposes.

The data is further segregated into:

- Microcredit fully utilized for the intended purpose
- Microcredit partially utilized for the intended purpose
- Microcredit not at all utilized for the intended purpose
- Microcredit obtained for consumption purposes in addition to the microcredit for microbusinesses
- Repayment behaviour of the male and female borrowers.

A comparative analysis of absolute figures and percentages was descriptively examined and illustrated through charts, tables, and diagrams. In the process of gathering operational data, demographic information such as name, age, gender, marital status, number of children, and educational attainment was also collected. Nonetheless, the demographic data has not indicated any substantial influence on the spending behaviour of the borrowers.

4.6 Scale refinement and validation

4.6.1 Refinement and validation of missing data

The author did not encounter the issue of missing data due to the utilization of three data collection methods: (i) visits to the borrowers, (ii) visits to the bank branch, and (iii) telephone calls to the managers. The author's involvement in the initial two methods clarified the issue of missing data at the moment of response. In the third method, the managers conveyed their insights on microcredit, along with their field experiences and personal observations regarding borrowers' ability to invest modest sums for income generation, asset creation, and loan repayment.

4.6.2 Asymmetrical response pattern

Irregular response patterns observed in the analysis included straight-lining, diagonal lining, and alternating extreme pole responses. No notable suspicious response patterns were detected in the replies of the borrowers or managers. The managers regarded themselves as representatives of the bank–MFI with which they are affiliated, and they completed the questionnaire with meticulous care and attention.

4.6.3 Outliers

The questionnaire did not include closed-ended questions requiring responses such as 'I agree', 'I strongly agree', or 'I strongly disagree'. The questions were direct and necessitated only numerical responses that borrowers or managers could provide candidly. Consequently, the responses accurately reflected the population, and all commonly identified outliers were preserved in the study. The results were meticulously assessed, revealing that the outliers had minimal impact on the analytical outcomes.

4.6.4 Data distributions

The approach was fundamentally a non-parametric statistical method that does not require the data to conform to a normal distribution. Nonetheless, it was confirmed that the data does not significantly deviate from normality through arithmetical analysis. The data was characteristically representative and gathered from a randomly selected area, assigning equal significance to each question, with no questionnaires or numerical values omitted to prevent skewness. The responses exhibited a standard flow, and the figures were precise. The responses regarding the amount of loan acquired, the outstanding loan to be repaid, and the amount of loan taken for consumption purposes were meticulously verified against passbooks and bank records to prevent discrepancies.

4.7 Research instrument

The study variables for the lender perception survey included ten financial performance indicators from the conceptual framework proposed by the author. The indicators accessing the financial performance of MFIs operating in India are elaborated below.

4.7.1 Lender performance indicators

a) Reduce non-performing assets (NPA)

RBI Circular No. RBI/2012-13/64 UBD.BPD.(PCB) MC No. 3/ 09.14.000/2012-13, dated 14 July 2012, defines NPAs as those that no longer generate bank income. Previously, 'Past Due' determined an asset's NPA status. Credit that has been 'past due' for a certain period was considered an NPA. Past due means 30 days past the due date. Since 31 March 2001, the term has been calculated from the payment due date instead of the 'past due' date. 1. From the year ended 31 March 2004, '90 days' overdue rules for NPA identification were implemented to align with international best practices and increase transparency. The lending managers wanted to reduce microcredit portfolio NPAs and maintain the institution's financial stability.

b) Poverty reduction

Microfinance is regarded as one of the most promising and economical instruments in the battle against global poverty. Over its three-decade trajectory, microfinance has served as a vehicle for enhanced livelihoods, benefiting nearly 100 million households through increased incomes. The sector has expanded under the influence of regulatory mandates and policy interventions directing its growth trajectory. Microfinance serves as a catalyst for change in the pursuit of Sustainable Development Goals by alleviating poverty and fostering self-employment opportunities.

c) Active borrowers

The active borrower base of an organization comprises the number of borrowers or entities with an outstanding loan balance or those obligated to repay any portion of the organization's gross loan portfolio. All loan products are aimed at the institution's active borrowers. Despite having obtained multiple loans from the same MFI, borrowers are recorded as a singular entity in the financial records.

d) Return on assets

The return on assets (ROA) for an organization is determined by the net operating income, after tax deductions, relative to the average assets. The ratio illustrates the organization's capacity to enhance profitability through the management of its total assets (Microfinance Information Exchange Glossary). The ratio signifies the firm's capacity to generate earnings from its assets, specifically the amount of rupees earned for each rupee of controlled assets. This is a premier metric for assessing profitability among banks and MFIs (Hubert Tchuigoua 2014; Narwal et al. 2015). ROA is a financial performance metric that indicates both profit margin and organizational efficiency (Kharti 2014).

4.7.2 Borrower perception attributes

In the borrower conceptual clarity, five research attributes were utilized to elucidate the differences in borrowers' perceptions regarding the achievement of the financial goals of the MIFs. These perceptions were noted during interactions with the borrowers. They seem to diverge from the lenders' perspective previously discussed. The five attributes were accessibility to get a loan, loan products, enhanced household financial status, elevated status of women within the household, and opportunities to fulfil social obligations. Detailed explanations follow below.

a) Accessibility to get a loan

The borrowers strongly desire that the loan be readily accessible with minimal paperwork. The MFIs must be accessible to borrowers without requiring endorsements from acquaintances, local leaders, brokers, or intermediaries. Access to financial support enables them to secure loans as needed and repay them when financially feasible. The borrowers are willing to repay; however, stringent deadlines may impede their ability to fulfil routine business activities and attend to social and familial obligations. Accessibility, in their terminology, signifies the ease of obtaining and repaying the loan.

b) Loan products—adequacy of the loan amount

The borrower satisfaction regarding the obtained loan product from the affiliated MFI is a significant metric. It substantially influences the borrowers' perception of the financial performance of MFIs operating in India. The borrower's satisfaction is achieved when the loan products offered by the institution are flexible, adequate, and customizable regarding parameters such as loan size, repayment frequency, and purposes beyond income-generating activities, including emergencies, education, fairs, festivals, health, deaths, births, housing, and repairs.

c) Enhanced household financial status

The borrowers obtain loans from MFIs to enhance their financial status, enabling them to operate businesses, fulfil personal and social obligations, and repay the loans. Consequently, the MFI loan package must be structured to enhance the financial status of the borrowers, taking into account their socio-economic conditions, clan, caste, and locality. Enhanced household income alone will mitigate numerous poverty-related afflictions, impacting the borrowers' lives. Consequently, microcredit serves primarily as an instrument for borrowers to enhance their household financial status, quality of life, and social status; it takes them out of indebtedness and saves the borrowers from unregulated money lenders.

d) Elevated status of women within the household

A further perceived advantage of accessing microcredit has been an enhancement in the status of women borrowers within households. This enhanced status enables them to accurately assess the financial performance of the MFI with which they are affiliated. In numerous instances, it was observed that female borrowers transferred the loan amounts to their husbands and subsequently received funds from them to settle the monthly instalments. The women borrowers have gained greater authority in managing household finances and are now more inclined to enquire about their partners' business dealings and the allocation of funds for instalment repayments. It has enhanced the financial responsibility of both men and women within the household regarding savings and cash management.

e) Opportunities to fulfil social obligations

A further perceived advantage of engaging with the relevant MFI is the opportunity to meet social obligations extended to microfinance borrowers, which enhances their perception of the institution. MFIs offers opportunities for socialization, especially within self-help groups. Regular group meetings facilitate interactions among various group members and individuals within the same group. Socializing fosters loyalty, trust, and camaraderie among the borrowers, which profoundly influences their perception of the organization.

Chapter 5 presents the research findings, evaluates the assumption, and correlates them with the research objectives. The objective of the research was to examine how borrowers utilize microcredit for unintended purposes. The objectives of the microcredit lenders are elucidated in section 4.7.1 and are juxtaposed with the borrowers' perceptions and behaviours detailed in section 4.7.2. The NPA data of MFIs, along with the data gathered for the current research, was utilized to evaluate the assumptions and derive conclusions in the subsequent chapters.

The NPAs indicate the performance of the loan product. NPAs typically arise when borrowers fail to repay loans obtained from financial institutions. First, the circumstances primarily resulting in the borrower's failure to repay the loan are attributed to non-performance of the loan product, specifically the inadequate generation of income from the investment, either due to market conditions or a design flaw in the product. Second, the majority of NPAs in small loans arise from borrower commitments unrelated to business requirements. The borrower's social, health, and familial obligations compel the diversion of funds originally designated for business purposes to urgent personal and family requirements, consequently exacerbating the NPAs of MFIs in the context of microcredits. Chapter 5 commences with an analysis of NPAs in MFIs as part of the research findings.

In conclusion, a cross-sectional data set, comprising both qualitative and quantitative data, was obtained from primary and secondary sources at a specific point in time. The primary data was obtained from a field survey utilizing a structured and pre-tested questionnaire. Mixed (non-probability purposive) and multistage (four-stage) 'probability sampling techniques' were employed to select the target respondents (Kothari 2004). A stratified random sampling technique, proportionate to sample size, was utilized to select 100 respondents from two financing institutions: a branch of a public-sector bank and a state government-operated microfinance facility for the final analysis. Focus group discussions and key informant interviews were conducted for the purpose of triangulation. The secondary data comprises pertinent information gathered from various relevant offices, websites, and associated documents. Descriptive statistical analysis methods were utilized to examine the data gathered from primary and secondary sources. Descriptive statistics, including frequency and percentage, were employed for analysis of data collected from both primary sources and secondary sources.

The descriptive statistical methods applied in this work are simply the measures of central tendency, consisting of arithmetical mean, median, and mode. Also, the standard deviation is identified. Excel packages were used to calculate the mean, median, mode, and standard deviation after inputting the data collected from the field. These calculations were made separately for the public-sector bank and for the MFI, for 50 borrowers each and for the entire 100 borrowers at once. Errors were avoided by manually calculating using the formulas for mean, median, mode, and standard deviation.

The mean, median, and mode represent the three measurements of central tendency. The mean is the arithmetic average of a data set. This is calculated by aggregating the values of total observations, then dividing the sum by the number of observations. The median is the central value of a data collection when the numbers are organized in ascending or descending order. The mode is the value that appears most frequently in a data set, whereas the range denotes the difference between the maximum and minimum values within that data set.

The median is the value that divides a distribution into two equal parts. One section encompasses all values that are more than or equal to the median, while the other segment includes all values that are less than or equal to it. The median is the central value when the data set is arranged in ascending order. The median, dependent on the order of values, remains unchanged even if the largest number increases.

One may occasionally aim to determine the most representative value of a series or the value around which the biggest concentration of objects is found. We must identify the predominant social event or the unanticipated goal that necessitates the largest financial resources to sustain the family. In this instance, the mode is the most appropriate metric. The term 'mode' derives from the French phrase 'la mode', signifying the most fashionable values within a distribution, since it appears with the most frequency in the data set. The mode is the data value that appears with the highest frequency. Mode represents this.

The standard deviation formula is employed to determine the dispersion of specific data values. The standard deviation is defined as the dispersion of values from the mean average. A smaller standard deviation indicates that the values are closely clustered around their mean. Higher values indicate a greater distance from the mean value. The standard deviation value cannot be negative.

However, I do not attempt to confuse the readers with the mathematical interpretation of social spending and deviation from the intended purposes. With this understanding, let us now proceed to Chapter 5, which analyses the data and explains the results. These measures of central tendency are not fully used in this study. However, mean values are considered.

5
Findings of the Study

5.1 Introduction

The findings are derived from an analysis of data gathered from 100 borrowers across 2 institutions: a branch of a major public-sector bank and a state government microfinance institution primarily providing savings and micro-investment services to women's self-help groups (SHGs). The data is gathered from individual beneficiaries, instead of SHGs, as SHGs represent distinct subjects necessitating separate research with varied parameters and enquiries. Findings are also derived from the literature review that supports the assumptions and the utility of microcredit obtained by the borrowers.

5.2 Presentation of findings

The study findings are delineated into three distinct sets of observations and analyses pertaining to various categories, themes, or areas of examination. The primary emphasis of the analysis of the secondary data is the assessment of non-performing assets (NPAs) in banks and microfinance institutions (MFIs). This analysis investigates whether borrowers' allocation of loans to social expenditures has elevated NPAs in banks, thereby affecting their financial stability.

The second domain relates to the analysis of primary data. The data collected from the field, encompassing discussions with banks and focus group meetings, is examined and presented through graphs, percentages, and interpretations. It also links to the NPAs within the MFIs.

The third domain entails connecting the perspectives of lenders and borrowers, as previously detailed, and synthesizing definitive insights from the evidence-based comparisons to derive conclusions and

Microcredit Misallocation? P. Gargi Rao, Oxford University Press. © P. Gargi Rao 2026.
DOI: 10.1093/9780197910573.003.0005

recommendations. The concluding section of this chapter involves empirically evaluating the assumptions and correlating the results with the research objectives.

5.3 Non-performing assets (NPAs)

An asset is classified as non-performing when it no longer produces income for the bank. To be specific, an asset was classified as an NPA based on the principle of 'past due'. An NPA is defined as credit for which interest and/or principal instalments have been 'past due' for a designated duration. Funds are disbursed by the bank/MFI as a loan to a borrower; if the borrower fails to repay the loan, and efforts of recovery by the banks also fail, it will be classified as an NPA. If the loan is returned to the bank/MFI, it may be re-lent to the same borrower or another, generating interest on it. The lending activity proceeds in this manner. Consequently, the funds designated for lending fulfil their function of generating income or profit for the institution, thereby becoming a performing asset. When this asset is not returned by the loanee, it ceases to generate returns and consequently becomes an NPA.

It is often observed that there is a high perceived risk of small and microloans turning into NPAs as they are usually lent out to small and marginal borrowers who lack the capacity of repayment in the agreed time framework. The NPAs in microcredit institutions increased in absolute terms from ₹4,88,921 lakh in 2020–21 to ₹5,74,371 lakh in 2021–22, reflecting a growth of 17.47% (year-on-year), as demonstrated in Table 5.1.

Gross NPAs decreased to 2.8% of the total outstanding loans, amounting to ₹1,88,078.80 crore as of 31 March 2023, down from 3.8% of outstanding loans totalling ₹1,51,051.30 crore as of 31 March 2022 (year-on-year) (Table 5.1). A reduction in NPAs is observable across all regions during the fiscal year (FY) 2022–23 when the economic activities normalized post the COVID-19 pandemic of 2020. The total NPAs decreased across all regions, reflecting an overall reduction of 9%, from ₹5,743.71 crore in FY 2021–22 to ₹5,249.33 crore in FY 2022–23. These declines do not inherently indicate perfection.

Table 5.1 Percentage region-wise NPA level (₹ in lakhs)

Sr. no.	Region	2020–21		2021–22		2022–23	
		Gross NPA amount	NPA as percentage to loan o/s	Gross NPA amount	NPA as percentage to loan o/s	Gross NPA amount	NPA as percentage to loan o/s
1	Northern region	17,133	13.93	18,094	10.94	15,694	7.48
2	North-eastern region	28,366	20.07	27,458	11.62	22,486	5.76
3	Eastern region	115,889	4.47	118,293	3.35	100,010	2.50
4	Central region	52,551	20.83	63,650	19.57	49,739	9.71
5	Western region	32,917	10.01	38,566	8.58	35,396	5.15
6	Southern region	242,064	3.52	308,310	2.96	301,608	2.32
	All-India	**488,920**	**4.73**	**574,371**	**3.80**	**524,933**	**2.79**

Source: Compiled by the author with the data from the National Bank for Agriculture and Rural Development (NABARD).

The regional comparison of NPAs indicates that the eastern and southern regions maintain NPA levels below the national average. In FY 2022–23, the central region exhibited the highest NPA percentage at 9.71%, followed by the northern region at 7.48% and the north-eastern region at 5.76%. The central region recorded the highest percentage of NPAs during 2020–21 and 2021–22, at rates of 20.83% and 19.57%, respectively. Nevertheless, there was a decrease in 2022–23 to 9.71%, representing a reduction of nearly ten percentage points, necessitating a thorough investigation into this abrupt decline in NPAs. It may involve either the provision of additional loans resulting from policy modifications or the government's forgiveness of loans as part of their electoral commitments.

Observing NPA trends through an agency-wise comparison indicates a reduction in NPAs across commercial banks, regional rural banks (RRBs), and rural cooperative banks (RCBs) during FY 2022–23, with a notable decrease in cooperative banks from an NPA level of 13.29% as of 31 March 2022 to 6.15% as of 31 March 2023 (Fig. 5.2). Cooperative banks experienced a significant rise in NPAs during 2021–22, and the causes for this sharp increase and the subsequent decline in 2022–23 remain undetermined, warranting further investigation in this domain. As previously questioned, there must have been a loan adjustment and waiver as a political commitment to the micro debtors in the current or preceding year. The likely reason for the abrupt and significant decline in NPAs, especially among cooperative banks, could be articulated as follows. The cooperative banks are operated by the government and are not classified as scheduled commercial banks by the Reserve Bank of India. The government exerts significant control over cooperative banks; thus, government policy decisions can promptly alter the loan portfolio and the NPA portfolio of commercial banks (Fig. 5.1 and Tables 5.1 and 5.2).

There has been a national decline in NPAs, falling from 3.80% in FY 2021–22 to 2.79% in FY 2022–23. The agency-specific NPA levels indicate that RRBs demonstrated the lowest gross NPA at 2.48%, followed by commercial banks at 2.79% and cooperative banks at 6.15%. The southern states have shown greater resilience to shocks, with a gross NPA of 2.32%, compared to the central region's 9.71% and the northern region's 7.28% gross NPA. The exemplary performance of southern states is because of the existence of efficient SHG-promoting institutions

Table 5.2 Lender-wise NPAs

Institution	2019–20	2020–21	2021–22	2022–23
Non-banking financial company (NBFC)–MFIs	2.23	9.45	9.10	8.47
Banks	2.36	9.45	14.39	13.82
Small Finance Banks (SFBs)	2.49	16.64	12.80	11.17
NBFCs	11.25	10.48	5.37	3.17
Not-for-Profit (NFP) MFIs	3.09	9.76	9.55	9.71
Total	**3.99**	**10.77**	**11.60**	**10.31**

Source: Compiled by the author from NABARD data.

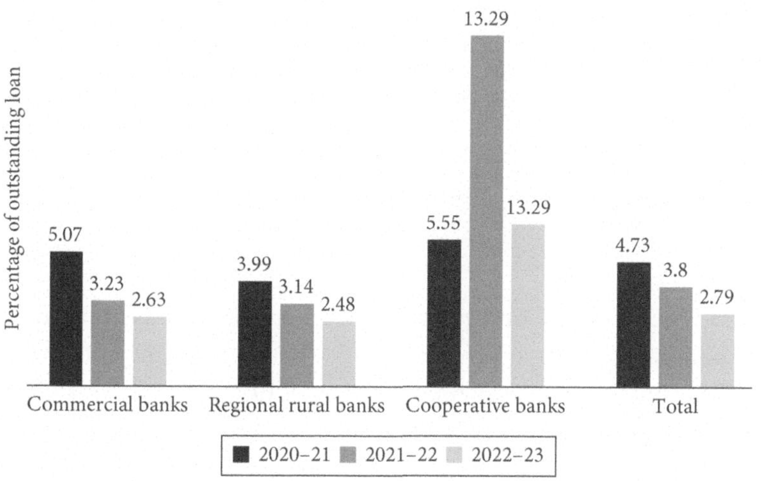

Fig. 5.1 NPA position of banks (SHGs–BPL) as a percentage during the period 2020–21 to 2022–23

Source: Prepared by the author from NABARD data.

(SHPIs)/partner agencies and the steadfast support of an active state government for SHGs that are below the poverty line (BLP). Regional disparities can be alleviated by addressing dormant accounts, purging data of inactive holders, supervising the record-keeping processes of SHGs, and emphasizing a capacity-building model with active involvement from state governments and banks.

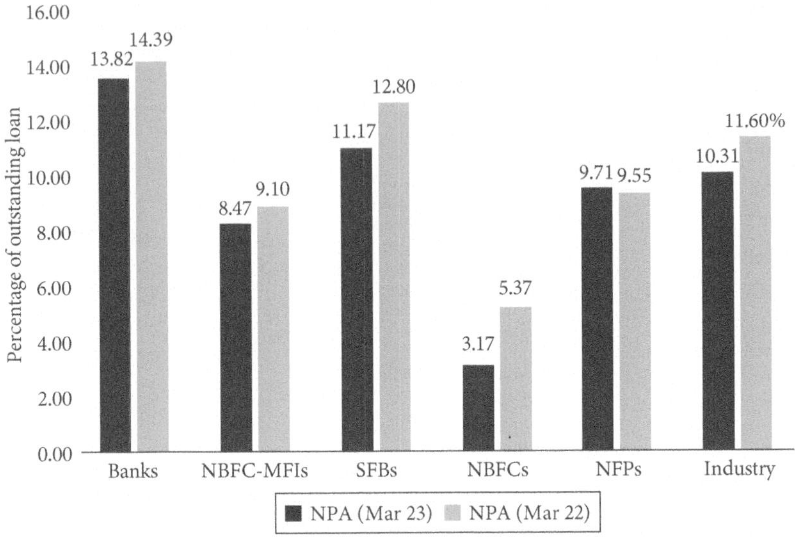

Fig. 5.2 NPA position of lenders (SHG–BLP) as a percentage during the period 2020–21 to 2022–23

Source: Mahila-Atmanirbhar Bharat (2022–23) *Status of Microfinance in India* (Mumbai: NABARD).

Based on the above observations, NPAs are significant indicators of loan non-payment by borrowers, particularly within the microcredit portfolio. Small and marginal borrowers fail to repay their small loans under three primary circumstances.

Scenario 1: when the borrowed funds fail to yield the required income for the borrower, it signals a deeper structural flaw in the economic activity. Typically, this arises when small investors or individual borrowers are unable to generate sufficient returns on their investments due to intense competition from large investors and multinational corporations, who possess substantial financial resources and economies of scale. These large entities can invest in advanced technology, employ superior marketing strategies, and utilize efficient distribution networks, all of which enable them to offer products or services at lower costs or with higher perceived value.

In contrast, smaller borrowers, often limited by access to resources, face significant challenges in matching the efficiency, reach, and appeal of larger players. This creates a competitive environment where minimal investments—such as those made by small businesses or individual borrowers—are overshadowed. The result is that small-scale borrowers struggle to generate sufficient returns to cover the costs of the borrowed capital, leading to a cycle of debt and financial strain. Addressing this issue requires a focus on policies and support systems that can level the playing field, providing smaller borrowers with the tools and resources needed to compete more effectively in an increasingly globalized market.

Scenario 2: a situation in which a borrower fails to repay a loan on time, or where the loan deteriorates in quality (meaning it is at risk of default), is often characterized by the misallocation of funds obtained from an MFI or bank. In such cases, rather than using the loan for its intended purpose—such as investing in a business, purchasing essential assets, or financing productive activities that generate income—the borrower diverts the funds to other unintended uses. These may include personal expenses, unproductive purchases, or social commitments, such as family ceremonies, medical expenses, or debt repayment for prior obligations.

This misallocation is typically symptomatic of financial strain, lack of financial literacy, or social pressures that lead the borrower to prioritize short-term needs over long-term financial planning. Where funds are diverted for non-productive purposes, they do not contribute to generating the income necessary to repay the loan, leading to a repayment crisis. This misuse can result in a cycle of debt as borrowers may need additional loans to cover the repayments of prior loans, further worsening their financial situation. Financial institutions, therefore, need to implement measures that support borrowers with proper guidance on fund allocation, income-generating strategies, and financial planning skills to help mitigate these risks and improve loan repayment outcomes.

Scenario 3: the issue also involves borrowers receiving informal assurances from political leaders or local authorities that the small loans they have taken will eventually be forgiven, either in full or in part. This apparent leniency may arise from political campaigns that utilize promises of loan waivers or relief programmes to attract specific voting demographics, especially in rural or economically disadvantaged regions. As a result, borrowers may anticipate, or at the very least wish for, the absolution of their debt in accordance with these assurances, so diminishing their motivation to prioritize repayment.

Additionally, borrowers frequently regard credit from public-sector banks or state government-operated microfinance firms as government assistance or welfare instead of legitimate financial responsibilities. This impression is particularly widespread in communities where subsidies, grants, or social welfare benefits are prevalent and may not necessitate repayment. Consequently, borrowers may perceive these loans as entitlements or gifts rather than as contractually binding obligations.

Such assumptions engender a problematic milieu for financial institutions as borrowers may default or postpone repayments, presuming there are no significant repercussions. Moreover, the expectation of loan waivers diminishes the discipline necessary for financial institutions to sustain robust portfolios. This cycle, fuelled by both political assurances and the view of loans as public benefits, calls for a need to clarify loan agreements, educate borrowers about financial obligations, and develop repayment frameworks that both support borrowers' success and ensure the sustainability of lending programmes.

5.4 Primary data analysis and findings

This study is founded on the empirical analysis of data gathered from a randomly selected cohort of 100 borrowers who have taken a total amount of ₹10.34 lakh in loans at an interest rate ranging between 14% and 14.6% per annum from two credit institutions: a branch of a public-sector bank and a state-run MFI. The borrowers from the public-sector bank branch comprise 32 women and 18 men from a semi-urban area of Hyderabad City, whereas the borrowers from the government's microfinance facility consist of 50 women from a rural area of Ranga Reddy District in Telangana (Balapur). The selected areas were randomly chosen from the list of regions and borrowers provided by the lending institutions, with no prior information about the borrowers other than their addresses and localities as supplied by the institutions. To overcome the existing bias, the project objectives and assumptions were not disclosed to the lending institutions or the borrowers.

The data was gathered using a comprehensive questionnaire designed to capture information on all necessary variables for the study. This questionnaire included both open-ended and close-ended questions, focusing on areas such as occupation, age, gender, education level, marital status, number of children, married children, unmarried daughters awaiting marriage, family income, essential expenses for family needs, loans taken for economic activities, and whether these loans were utilized for their intended purposes. It also collected details on overdue bank loans with interest, loan amounts spent on unintended purposes such as daily family expenses, loans obtained from other lenders, loans taken solely for consumption, and the adequacy of the loan amounts (Table 5.3).

An interactive engagement strategy was employed to gather objective data from borrowers instead of depending exclusively on conventional questioning techniques. Selected borrowers engaged in comprehensive discussions, acting as the principal source for data acquisition. Insights obtained from these discussions were later cross-verified with the borrowers to ensure consistency and correctness with the recorded questionnaire responses.

The gathered data was validated with the lending institutions to ensure precision and avert discrepancies. The focus was on the loan amount, the purpose of the loan, the late amount, and the repayment conduct of the borrowers. The NPAs of the lending institutions were also verified to encompass a segment of the delinquent microcredit from the borrowers. The credit institutions were interviewed to gather information about their comprehensive lending policies, recovery strategies employed during standard operations, and related constraints.

5.4.1 Impact of borrower age on loan diversion

Borrowers' age group influences both the eligibility for a loan and their repayment behaviour. IndusInd Bank has analysed the influence of age on credit.

How does age impacts your eligibility for personal loans?

a) Young borrowers (21–30 years): young borrowers frequently face challenges related to their limited credit history, which can significantly impact their loan eligibility. Without an established record of accomplishment of responsible credit use, banks and financial institutions may view these individuals as higher-risk borrowers. This perception stems from their short credit histories, which provide limited insight into their repayment habits as well as their often limited financial assets or savings to act as collateral or a safety net.

However, young borrowers are not entirely without options. If they can demonstrate a steady and reliable income—such as through stable employment or a long-term contract—and maintain a good credit score, they may still qualify for personal loans. An excellent credit score indicates prudent credit practices, including punctual payments and low debt levels, which can reduce the perceived risk for lenders. Moreover, young borrowers may gain advantage by collaborating with institutions that provide credit-building products or with lenders focused on youth and novice credit financing. These criteria can enhance their likelihood of obtaining funds, so progressively aiding them in establishing a favourable credit profile over time.

b) Middle-aged borrowers (31–50 years): individuals in their thirties and forties generally possess a better-developed credit history, reflecting a consistent record of financial prudence over time. After years of credit development, they typically demonstrate regular payment patterns, reduced debt-to-income ratios, and have a variety of credit kinds (including credit cards, auto loans, and mortgages), all of which enhance their creditworthiness. This financial maturity enhances their eligibility for personal loans and typically enables them to negotiate advantageous loan terms.

Additionally, individuals in this age range are more likely to have stable employment, often with greater career advancement and income levels than younger borrowers. Higher income and job security mean that lenders see less risk in extending credit as these borrowers are viewed as more likely to maintain steady repayments. Consequently, lenders may offer them better terms, including lower interest rates, extended repayment periods, or even higher loan amounts, as they are seen as lower risk.

Moreover, these borrowers are often able to leverage their established financial portfolios, which may include savings, retirement accounts, or investments, to secure competitive terms. This combination of a strong credit profile, stable income, and financial stability gives borrowers in their thirties and forties more flexibility in loan options, allowing them to make more financially advantageous borrowing decisions.

c) Older borrowers (51–60+years): the proximity to retirement age can significantly impact personal loan eligibility for older borrowers as lenders become more cautious about the borrower's future income stability and capacity to meet repayment obligations post-retirement. Since retirement typically leads to a reduction in monthly income, lenders may view these borrowers as higher risk due to potential difficulties in managing loan payments on a fixed income, such as pensions or social security.

To mitigate this perceived risk, financial institutions may impose stricter eligibility criteria, which could include requiring higher minimum income levels, additional collateral, or even a guarantor to secure the loan. Despite these challenges, many older borrowers do bring advantages to the table, such as a well-established credit history, indicating years of responsible credit usage, and substantial financial assets, such as real estate or retirement savings. These assets demonstrate financial maturity and can enhance creditworthiness.

However, the lender's focus on repayment capacity often still leads to more conservative loan terms. This may mean shorter repayment periods to ensure the loan is fully repaid before or soon after retirement or higher interest rates to offset the higher risk. In some cases, lenders may even limit loan amounts for older applicants, preferring to reduce the potential financial exposure. For older borrowers, securing favourable loan terms often requires highlighting their financial assets, supplemental retirement income streams, or potentially providing a co-signer, all of which can reassure lenders and facilitate better access to credit.

Consequently, the age-group data of borrowers was collected separately for the bank branch of the public-sector banks (BBPSB) across 50 cohorts and for the state government-operated MFIs

Table 5.3 Borrowers' age profile (BBPSB)

Age group	Classification	Percentage loan amount spent on social events
21–30	Young borrowers	47.00
31–50	Middle-aged borrowers	53.00
51–60+	Old-age borrowers	52.00

Source: Compiled by the author.

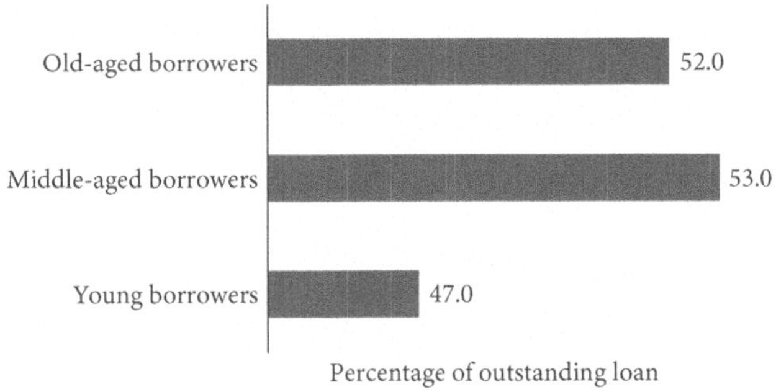

Fig. 5.3 The percentage loan amount spent on social needs by age group
Source: Prepared by the author.

across 50 cohorts. The SHG–MFI cohorts consisted exclusively of women, while the BBPSB comprised 18 men and 32 women. The collected data was analysed with consideration of the influence of age on borrowers' repayment behaviour (Fig. 5.3).

The above data represents the borrowers from the BBPSB. The age demographic of borrowers has not significantly influenced the misallocation of loans intended for income generation.

Young borrowers allocated around 53% of the loan amount towards income-generating activities, while a little less than half (47%) was directed towards social expenditures. In contrast, middle-aged borrowers dedicated a relatively larger share (i.e. 53% of the entire loan amount) towards social expenditure and only 47% of their loan amount on income-generating activities or for investment purposes. Senior borrowers did not demonstrate any notable differences compared to their counterparts in the middle-aged group. The elderly borrowers expended only

1% (52%) less on social events compared to their middle-aged counterparts. Besides the behavioural data representation, the younger borrowers articulated their enterprising nature and expressed a desire to utilize the funds for income generation. They expended significantly less (6 percentage points) on the social events compared to their middle-aged counterparts.

Middle-aged borrowers have children of marriageable age as well as school- and college-aged offspring, and older parents as dependents, in contrast to other age demographics. They are engaged in social life, relationships, and the preservation of familial values, customs, beliefs, and religion as well as being concerned about social admonition and the stigma associated with failing to fulfil social obligations.

While younger borrowers possess social responsibilities, they have young children and are capable of declining certain commitments, demonstrating a readiness to confront challenges that their older counterparts could not. The senior cohort in the elderly demographic possesses commitments comparable to those of their middle-aged counterparts, resulting in similar expenditures on social events.

Figure 5.4 and Table 5.4 illustrate the data of 50 cohorts who have obtained loans from the state-operated MFI. All borrowers from this MFI were women aged 21–50. No elderly cohorts existed as were present in the cohort of the BBPSB. To facilitate comparative analysis, borrowers were categorized into two age groups: one a young cohort (21–30 years), while the other was middle-aged (31–50 years).

The younger borrowers of MFIs allocated a significantly lesser proportion (41%) of the borrowed funds to social expenditures, whereas their middle-aged counterparts allocated over half of the loan (53%) to social events. The younger borrowers demonstrated their dedication to

Table 5.4 Percentage loan amount spent on social events by borrowers of government-run MFIs

Age group	Classification	Percentage spent
21–30	Young borrowers	41.00
31–50	Middle-aged borrowers	53.00

Source: Compiled by the author.

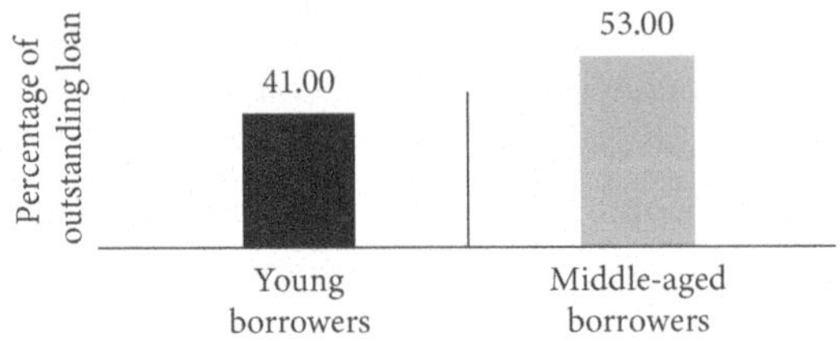

Fig. 5.4 The percentage loan amount spent on social events by the borrowers of government-run microfinance institutions
Source: Prepared by the author.

investing capital for returns, allocating a substantial portion (59%) of their loans to income-generating activities, despite experiencing losses in these investments. The middle-aged counterparts allocated 12% more (53%) of their resources to social events compared to their younger counterparts. Middle-aged borrowers were also influenced by their husbands regarding earnings and borrowings, which prevented them from fully investing the loan funds in the intended activities.

5.4.2 A comparison of borrowers' age groups in diverting the loan to social spending

To compare the influence of borrowers' age on loan diversion, age was categorized into smaller groups, as indicated in Table 5.5. No symmetry exists among borrowers from the two different financial institutions. Borrowers aged 30–35, 35–40, and 40–45 from the public-sector bank branch expended less on social events compared to their counterparts from the government's MFI. Borrowers from public-sector bank branches aged 25–30 and 45–50 significantly diverted funds from their loans for social expenditures, with 47% and 72%, respectively, contrary to the intended loan purposes (Fig. 5.5).

The analysis of age groups reveals a distinct impact on borrowing from lending institutions and the subsequent repayment. The misallocation of loans to unproductive and unintended purposes appears to be predominantly age-neutral, and it cannot be generalized that younger individuals

Table 5.5 Percentage loan amount diverted towards social events by the borrowers of both the institutions

Age group	GRMFI	BBPSB
25–30	41.90	47.00
30–35	48.60	42.00
35–40	53.60	52.00
40–45	63.90	53.00
45–50	66.70	72.00
50–55	0.00	62.00
55–60	0.00	0.00

Source: Compiled by the author.

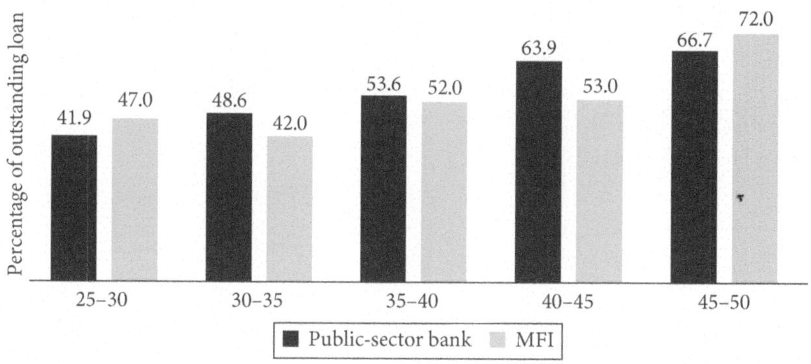

Fig. 5.5 The percentage loan amount diverted towards social events
Source: Prepared by the author.

misallocate loans while older individuals do not or vice versa. Minor differences are observed in certain young cohorts; however, these cannot be generalized. Poverty, low family income, consumption needs, familial obligations, social responsibilities, and the fear of social ostracism significantly influenced loan diversion, whereas age was not a pertinent factor. Nevertheless, younger borrowers demonstrated the audacity to confront societal admonitions and utilize the borrowed funds for their intended purpose. A diversion of smaller sums from this young cohort is observed but not the investment of the entire loan in economic activities (Fig. 5.6 and Table 5.6).

Table 5.6 Educational levels of borrowers from BBPSBs

Educational level	Percentage loan amount spent on social events
Primary	51.70
Secondary	52.80
No education	50.00

Source: Compiled by the author.

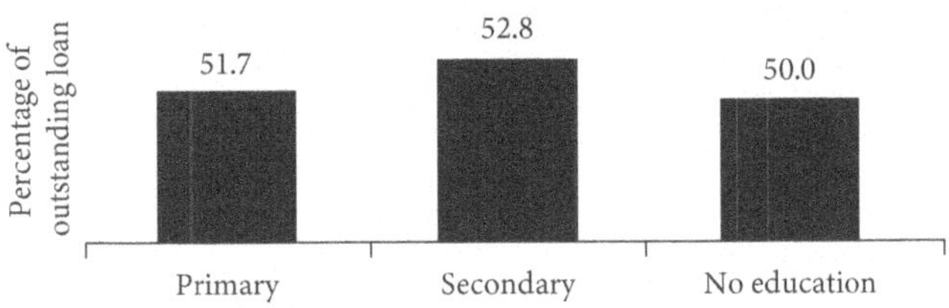

Fig. 5.6 The percentage of educational-level bank branch of the public-sector bank (BBPSB)
Source: Prepared by the author.

5.4.3 Education levels of the borrowers

The educational background of the borrowers was the subsequent data point that was gathered and analysed in this research. The educational attainment of a borrower does not significantly influence the misallocation of loans to unintended purposes by the borrowers. Nearly all borrowers, with the exception of 1 in 100, possessed an education level of secondary or lower. The activities conducted by borrowers, such as vegetable vending, operating a barber shop, ironing clothes, street vending of garments, and assisting an electrician or plumber, did not necessitate advanced educational qualifications, and other minor enterprises did not demonstrate any influence on borrower behaviour.

All 50 borrowers from the BBPSB allocated over 50% of their loans to social expenditures. Notably, illiterate borrowers restricted their allocation to a minimum of 50%, whereas borrowers with secondary education diverted the highest proportion (52.8%) of their loans to social spending, while their counterparts allocated slightly less (51.7%). Furthermore, the data gathered, along with interviews conducted with borrowers from

Table 5.7 Educational levels of borrowers and percentage loan amount spent on social events (state-run MFIs)

Educational level	Percentage loan amount spent on social events
Primary	49.40
Secondary	42.10
No Education	69.40

Source: Compiled by the author.

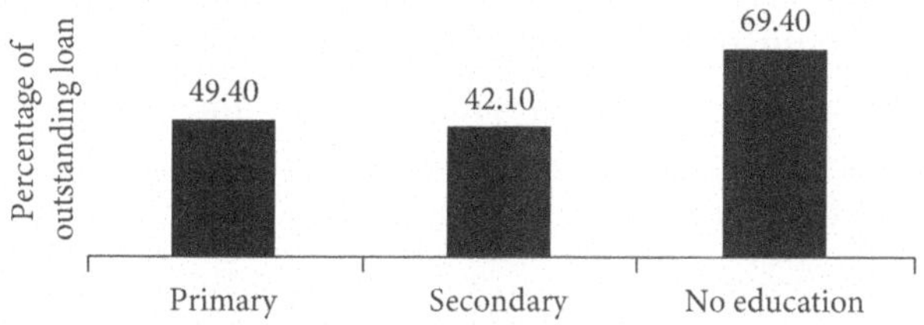

Fig. 5.7 Educational level and loan spent (state-run microfinance institution)
Source: Prepared by the author.

the public-sector bank branch, indicated that the educated individuals were more cognizant and capable of articulating issues related to income inadequacy, poverty, and social obligations. They demonstrated slightly greater courage in reallocating the loans to social initiatives than their uneducated counterparts. Nonetheless, the study indicates that all aforementioned borrowers misallocated funds for social expenditures, regardless of their educational attainment, and education did not significantly assist the borrowers in utilizing the funds solely for their intended purpose (Fig. 5.7).

All borrowers from the state government's MFI were female. The educational attainment of borrowers did not demonstrate any substantial impact on their spending behaviour. The spending on social events among borrowers ranged from 69.40% to 42.10%, revealing that education level does not have a significant relation to borrowers' behaviour. Nevertheless, the borrowers lacking education allocated a substantial portion of their loan (69.40%) to social expenditures, whereas women with secondary education exhibited a markedly lower allocation

(42.10%). Many impoverished, illiterate women perceived the loan as a subsidy as it originated from a government MFI that possessed asymmetric information regarding the allocation of funds for income generation. Literacy, low income, and familial obligations compelled this group of female borrowers to allocate a greater portion of funds to social expenditures compared to their counterparts with secondary education, who diverted only 42.10% of the loan.

Furthermore, of the 50 interviewed borrowers from the government's MFI, 31 (62%) possessed secondary education, 18 (36%) had primary education, 5 (10%) were literate, and merely 1 (2%) was illiterate. They possessed the ability to read, write, and sign in the vernacular.

In both the government microcredit programme and public-sector bank services, women with secondary education surpassed men in number. One of the female borrowers possessed a university degree. Due to insufficient data, we cannot generalize that educated women effectively utilize bank loans; however, this female borrower, a university graduate and professional photographer, secured a loan of ₹20,000, of which only ₹5,000 remains to be repaid to the bank. The borrower had not misallocated the loan obtained for productive purposes to unintended uses. The borrower was 35 years old, married, and had one child in school and three dependants. The bank found her repayment behaviour satisfactory and was prepared to offer her a second loan, if necessary, contingent upon the borrower's performance. However, as previously stated, repayment habits and fund diversion cannot be deduced purely from the educational attainment of an individual respondent.

To support the previously indicated viewpoint, three additional examples may be examined. An illiterate individual, a painter, and two individuals with primary education each obtained a loan of ₹10,000, which they only invested in their respective companies, without diverting the funds for any other societal purpose. Thus, it appears that loan repayment behaviour or the misallocation of loans to unproductive and unanticipated ends is not influenced by education and cannot be attributed to the borrowers' literacy levels.

The findings revealed that neither education nor age had a significant impact on the reallocation of funds from unexpected uses to social expenditures by borrowers in both the BBPSU and government MFI. Conversely, the borrowers' poverty, low income, familial responsibilities, and societal customs strongly impacted their decision to allocate funds for social expenditures.

5.4.4 Activity of the borrowers

The activities of borrowers disclose their economic engagements. These also disclose whether the financing institutions have identified a borrower for microcredit. The borrowers from Institution 1, a public-sector bank branch, disclosed the activities they had undertaken and were currently engaged in during the research conducted by the investigator. All borrowers from the government MFI disclosed that they obtained loans for small business endeavours. They did not elaborate on their activities as the other group of borrowers did.

Figure 5.8 above reveals that 21 borrowers, representing 42% of the total, were street vendors selling various items on the streets. Eight per cent of the borrowers sold idly: vada, dosa, tea, bread, and various other quick snacks. Twenty per cent were vegetable vendors, another 20%

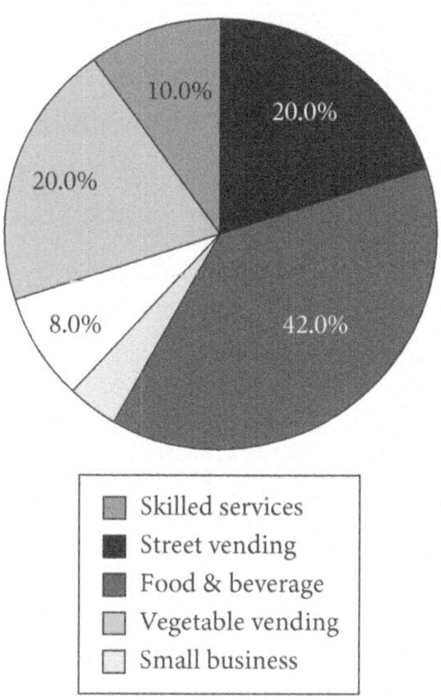

Fig. 5.8 Activity institution (BBPSB)
Source: Prepared by the author.

provided services such as electricians, plumbers, cobblers, and watch repairers, while 10% engaged in small business activities.

While the borrowers from a government-operated microfinance entity did not disclose their specific activities, observations during field visits indicated their involvement in street vending, vegetable sales, roadside textile commerce, and minor enterprises. One aspect requires clarification in this context. Institution 2 typically provided credit facilities via SHGs. The SHGs subsequently extend loans to their members, many of whom were engaged not in business ventures but in ancillary agricultural and traditional occupations that necessitated minimal investment. SHGs were not purposefully examined, as they constitute a distinct and autonomous subject. Consequently, it was challenging to identify individual borrowers directly from the MFI, ultimately resulting in the identification of 50 female borrowers who disclosed their engagement in small business activities.

The borrowers' activities explain that they were not only diminutive and necessitating minimal investments but also that they typically encountered challenges related to urbanization; the burgeoning shopping mall culture; climate change (especially for those involved in street and vegetable vending); mechanization; and occasionally social unrest, bandhs, hartals, and elections. Small and minor enterprises operated by women encountered numerous challenges stemming from familial obligations, admonitions from male relatives, childbearing responsibilities, personal health issues, and the health of in-laws, spouses, and children, as well as travel between in-laws and parental residences, among other demands.

The microfinance findings of the International Labour Organization (ILO) for women are noteworthy:

> Studies show that husbands or male family members sometimes make all loan decisions for women. Different literacy, property rights, and social attitudes concerning women may restrict impact outside the home. Microfinance is challenging for rural residents. The burden of loan repayment may also strain women. Access to finance affects how men and women in the same family work and between different-return activities. Evidence suggests that microcredit increases women's and girls' workload but may offset this with increased household

decision-making equality. Institutionally, MFIs may lose women clients when they migrate upscale for better profits or become commercial banks. The commercial justification for targeting female borrowers must be emphasized while strengthening MFI initiatives to reach women.

5.4.5 Analysis of household income of the borrowers

The annual household income of the borrower and the annual expenses necessary to sustain the family enabled us to correlate an individual's financial needs with the available monetary resources to fulfil those needs. When family expenditures cross the total household means, the individual must either acquire funds from alternative sources or augment their income to satisfy basic minimum necessities. The target population for this work consists of microcredit borrowers from the lower socio-economic classes. The Government of Telangana, Department of Consumer Affairs, Food, and Civil Supplies, has raised the income threshold for eligibility of BPL families (priority households) to ₹1.50 lakh per annum in rural areas and ₹2 lakh per annum in urban areas. The limit on land ownership has been raised to 3.5 acres of irrigated land and 7.5 acres of non-irrigated land. It was specified that land income will be considered as a criterion for the issuance of BPL cards. Keeping this in view, let us now examine the income, family size, amount required to run the family, and amount diverted from the loans towards social commitments.

Some of the findings from the research of other scholars and field interviews indicated that most borrowers from BPL families are unable to invest small loan amounts productively as their subsistence needs take precedence over business considerations (Fig. 5.9).

This chart shows how family size affected the overall expenditure on social events. In a developing country like India, where a family size of four is considered to be the new normal, around 44.7% of the household income is spent on social events to satisfy their social and societal needs. Similarly, if we consider a household of five members, it is highly probable that there are three dependents and two earning members and that more than 50% of their household income is spent on social events. With

Table 5.8 Income, family size, and percentage loan amount spent on social events (in ₹1,000)

Income level and social spending (BBPSB)		
Family size	**Mean household income (in ₹1,000)**	**Percentage loan amount spent on social events**
1	100.17	68.3
2	104.00	47.1
3	97.00	52.0
4	108.33	44.4
5	95.00	57.8
6	101.00	56.7

Source: Compiled by the author.

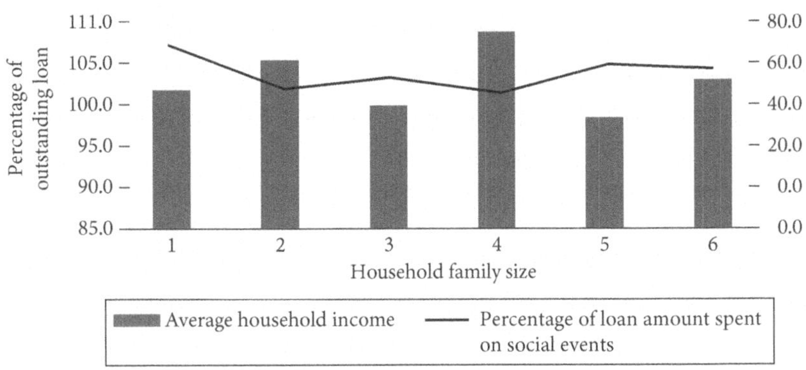

Fig. 5.9 Family size and amount spent on social events
Source: Prepared by the author.

the growing trend of a rise in only two-member households, spending on social gatherings such as small festivals, small events, and functions has been on the rise, and it can be clearly stated that around 52% of their annual income is spent on unintended economic activities.

Tables 5.8 and 5.9 clearly indicate that both family income and the funds necessary to satisfy minimum family needs fall below the BPL income thresholds. The Government of Telangana defines BPL income as ₹1.50 lakh per annum in rural regions and ₹2 lakh per annum in urban regions. The borrowers from the BBPSB had a mean family income of

Table 5.9 Income levels and family requirements

Institution		Family requirement	Yearly household income	Loan taken
BBPSB	Mean	140,800	102,240	11,100
GRMFI		133,000	121,320	10,000

Source: Compiled by the author.

₹1,02,240, while the family expenditure requirement was ₹1,40,800. They secured a mean loan of ₹11,100 for investment, profit generation, loan repayment, and reinvestment to sustain the business cycle. No mathematics can explain how an investment of ₹11,100 can generate income to fill the gap of ₹38,560 (₹1,40,800 – ₹1,02,240 = ₹38,560), pay the monthly equated instalment to the bank, and reinvest the original capital amount again.

The government-operated MFI primarily addressing women's microfinance requirements reported a mean family income of ₹1,21,300, This income is significantly below the BPL threshold. The interviewees asserted a requisite minimum mean income of ₹1,33,000. This is lower than the income suggested by the government for the BPL threshold. The female borrowers from this government MFI secured a mean loan amount of ₹9,580. The borrowers were anticipated to escape poverty by investing the loan, generating profits, repaying the loans, and fulfilling personal expenses, including social obligations. If funds allocated for business purposes were diverted, the borrower would likely prioritize immediate social needs to avoid any associated stigma. Borrowers from this income bracket and social class were more concerned about their 'Badnaami' than incurring debt to the bank.

The circumstances of the 100 borrowers from the 2 institutions were indistinguishable from those of the borrowers evaluated separately from each institution. The mean household income of the 100 borrowers was ₹1,01,780. The mean monetary requirement was ₹1,36,900. The average credit acquired by these borrowers was ₹10,340. All the borrowers' families were BPL families and were expected to come above the poverty line by investing the credit taken from the MFIs.

5.4.6 Analysis of loan utilization

This is the primary focus of this work, wherein the author seeks to ascertain the utilization of microcredit by borrowers.

For analytical purposes, the utilization of credit is classified into two categories. The primary objective of the loan is that the loan provided by the MFI is intended for the borrower to invest in an activity specified by the lender, generate income exceeding expenses from that activity, satisfy daily consumption requirements, repay the principal and interest to the MFI, and reinvest the funds. The cycle continues, and the borrower is expected to escape poverty or exceed the poverty threshold.

The second category is the unintended allocation of the loan funds by the borrower towards immediate social and customary needs rather than investing in the designated income-generating activity. The author observed that borrowers allocated credit to various social, religious, customary, and sustenance needs rather than investing it in business to generate sustainable income for livelihood.

The utility of the loan amount was examined across four categories, correlating it with the total loan acquired as well as the family's needs and income levels:

a) The loan amount was completely consumed on business activities or designated purposes. The borrowers did not misallocate any funds from the loan obtained but invested entirely in the designated economic or business activity.
b) The loan amount was entirely utilized for an unintended objective. The borrower completely allocated the loan to unintended social obligations without investing in the designated economic activity or business for which the credit was provided: the misallocation.
c) The loan partially utilized the funds for the identified economic activity while redirecting the remainder to unintended purposes.
d) The loan was partially invested in the intended purpose while the rest was allocated to the identified economic activity or business.

Categories (c) and (d) appear identical. Nonetheless, the categories distinguish between the amount or percentage of the loan allocated for the intended activity and the amount or percentage of the loan

Table 5.10 Loan utility by the borrowers of BBPSBs

Category	Percentage	₹
Loan fully used for unintended purpose	17.11	95,000
Loan fully used for business	19.82	110,000
Loan partially used for an unintended purpose	36.49	202,500
Loan partially spent on business	26.58	147,500

Source: Compiled by the author.

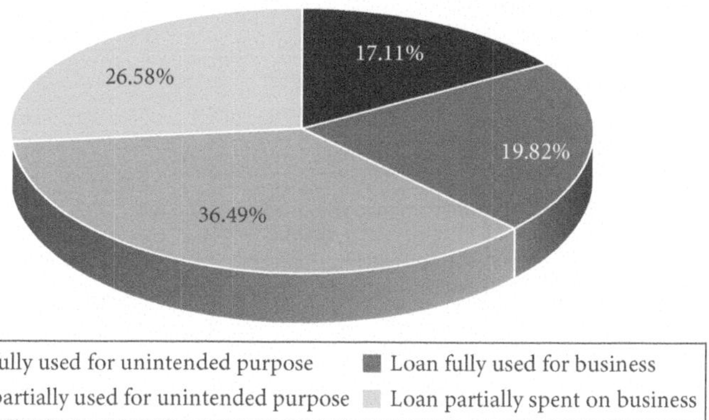

Fig. 5.10 Loan utility (BBPSB)
Source: Prepared by the author.

misappropriated for unintended activities by the same individual (Fig. 5.10 and Table 5.10).

Table 5.7 and Fig. 5.8 elucidate that the 50 borrowers from Institution 1 employed the loan amounts variably. Out of a total loan amount of ₹555,000 obtained by 50 borrowers from the institution, 10 borrowers completely utilized ₹110,000 (19.82% of the loan) for the intended purpose, while 7 borrowers fully expended approximately 17.11% (or ₹95,000) on unintended purposes. An amount of ₹2,02,500, representing 36.49% of the total loan acquired, was partially allocated for unintended purposes, while ₹1,47,500, accounting for 26.58% of the total loan, was partially utilized for business purposes. In contrast, of the ₹5,50,000 loan acquired by the 50 borrowers, only ₹2,57,500, representing 46.39% of the total loan, was allocated for business purposes, while the remaining 53.60% was utilized for unintended purposes, either partially or entirely.

Table 5.11 Loan utility for different unintended expenditures (BBPSBs)

Purpose	Percentage of use	Amount in ₹
Food	6.05	18,000
Clothing	0.67	2,000
Health	6.72	20,000
Marriage of children	12.77	38,000
Education	4.54	13,500
Death in the family	3.70	11,000
Other social commitments	28.74	85,500
Gifts	2.86	8,500
Religious	16.47	49,000
Festivals	13.78	41,000
Pilgrimages	3.36	10,000
Repaying local debts	0.34	1,000
Total	**100.00**	**297,500**

Source: Compiled by the author.

Consequently, 40 out of the 50 borrowers, representing 80%, allocated 53.60% of the loan for unintended purposes.

The activities on which these borrowers spent the loan amount are discussed here with the help of Fig. 5.11 and Table 5.11.

The borrowers utilized the loan for sustenance, apparel, health care, children's marriages, education, bereavement, various social obligations, presents, religious pursuits, festivals, and pilgrimages. An examination of the borrowers' spending behaviours reveals that they possessed numerous immediate obligations and necessities that took precedence over investing funds, awaiting income generation, and subsequently fulfilling social commitments (Fig. 5.12).

Among the expenditures, social commitments (28.74%), religious expenditures (16.47%), festivals (13.78%), and children's marriages (12.77%) assumed greater significance compared to other expenditures such as health (6.72%), food (6.05%), and education (4.54%). Health and education services are provided at no cost to BLP individuals and to children in primary and pre-primary schools; consequently, significant expenditures in these sectors were not observed. The sentiments and stigmatization associated with poverty, along with traditional responsibilities

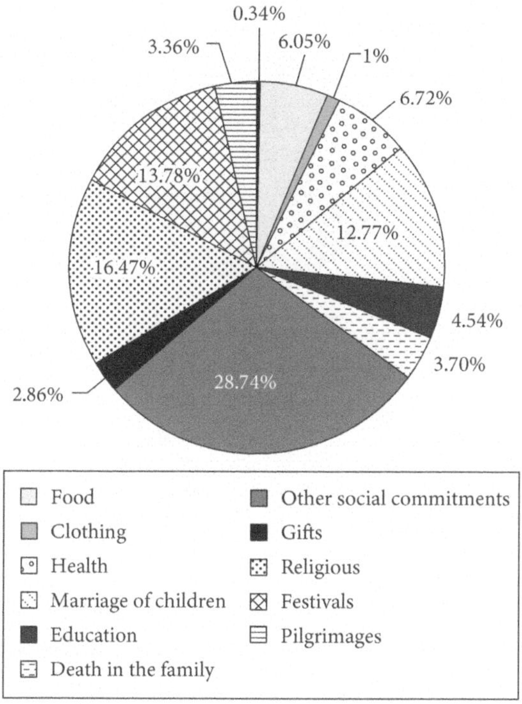

Fig. 5.11 Loan utility for unintended purposes
Source: Prepared by the author based on data collected from the field.

Table 5.12 Loan utility of borrowers from GRMFIs

S. no.	Purpose	Amount (₹)	Percentage
1	Fully spent on business	13,000	3
2	Fully spent on unintended purposes	25,000	5
3	Partially spent on business	239,000	50
4	Partially spent on unintended purposes	202,000	42
	Total	**479,000**	**100**

Source: Prepared by the author based on data collected from the field.

and commitments, compelled borrowers to allocate more resources to these areas rather than investing in sustainable solutions to poverty.

All 50 women borrowers from the government-managed MFI allocated only 3% of their loans entirely to business; 5% of the loans were

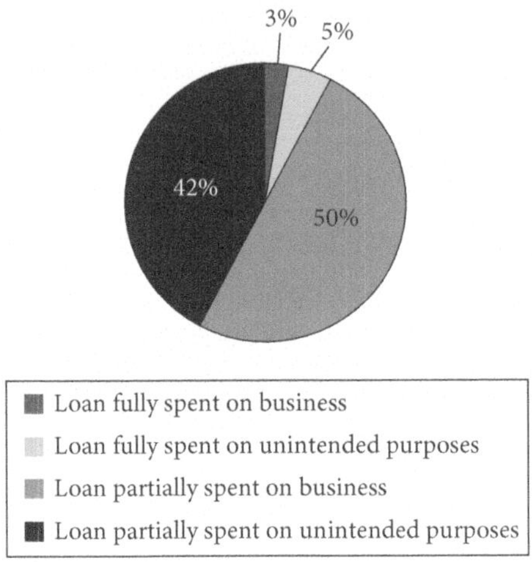

Fig. 5.12 Loan utility by borrowers of the SRMFI
Source: Prepared by the author.

completely diverted to unintended purposes, while 50% of the loans were partially utilized for business and 42% were partially expended on unintended purposes. Consequently, 47% of the loan was allocated for unintended purposes. The borrowers from Institution 2 had not repaid approximately 98% of their loans.

Borrowers from both institutions, which operate in distinct locations, lack any connection; however, they share the commonality of poverty and the misallocation of loans for unintended purposes not supported by the MFI (Fig. 5.13 and Table 5.13).

A comparison of the 100 interviewed borrowers from the 2 MFIs indicates no significant difference in their loan utilization behaviour. Both diverted funds designated for business and economic activities aimed at generating sustainable income towards unintended and unproductive ends. Social, religious, cultural, and customary obligations superseded their dedication to financial investment, income generation, and poverty alleviation. The notable disparity is that women borrowers from the government-managed MFI allocated only 3% of their loans entirely to business, whereas their counterparts from the BBPSB dedicated 19.82% of their loans fully to the specified activities. Furthermore, 48 borrowers from both institutions secured consumption loans, whereas 52 borrowers refrained from obtaining any loans beyond those for economic

Table 5.13 Loan utility by all 100 borrowers from both the institutions (in ₹1,000)

S. no.	Purpose	BBPSB	GRMFI	Total (₹1,000)
1	Fully spent on business	110.0 (19.82%)	13.0 (3%)	123.0 (11.89%)
2	Fully spent on unintended purposes	95.0 (17.11%)	25.0 (5%)	120.0 (11.61%)
3	Partially spent on business	147.5 (26.58%)	239.0 (50%)	386.5 (37.38%)
4	Partially spent on unintended purpose	202.5 (36.49%)	202.0 (42%)	404.5 (39.12%)
	Total	**555.0**	**479.0**	**1,034.0 (100%)**
	Consumption loans: YES	**26**	**16**	**42**
	Consumption loans: NO	**24**	**34**	**58**

Source: Compiled by the author.

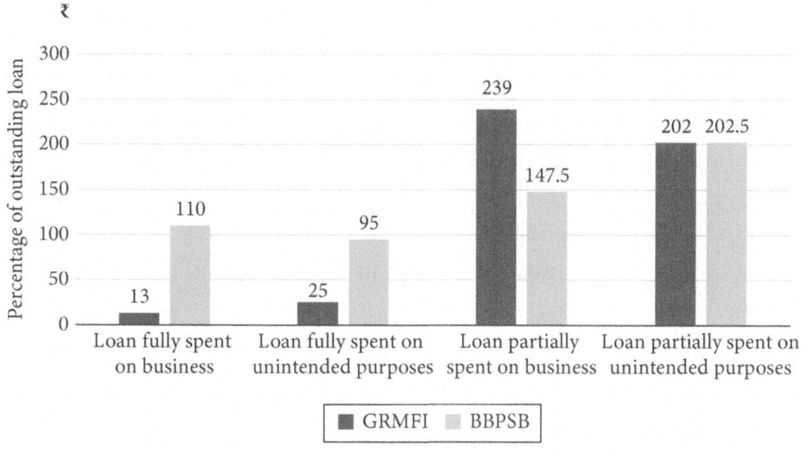

Fig. 5.13 Loan utility by all 100 borrowers from both the institutions (₹,000)

Source: Prepared by the author.

activities. However, a unified national policy framework for the provision of consumption loans to BPL households remains absent. Nonetheless, this supplementary loan did not inhibit them from reallocating funds.

MFIs are conventionally regarded as crucial in alleviating poverty by offering diverse financial services (microcredit, savings, and additional services) to individuals involved in small and microeconomic ventures who lack the means to adopt new technologies and initiate business activities independently; thus, they are often referred to as 'small banks'. The primary aim of this work is to identify the factors influencing loan diversion among small-scale group borrowers from two microcredit lending institutions. A pre-tested structured questionnaire was employed to collect data from 100 individuals involved in small enterprises, services, and caste-based activities, utilizing the multistage sampling method. Descriptive statistics were employed to analyse the collected data. The study indicated that out of the sample households, 80 (80%) diverted funds to the extent of 50.72% for unintended purposes, while the remaining 20 (20%) did not divert their loan to unintended goals. On the basis of sample data collected, keeping other variables constant, it can be inferred that the majority of the sample failed to utilize the loan amount towards expanding businesses or investing in income-generating activities. The diversions were undertaken to fulfil their social obligations. The findings demonstrate that the loan's purpose, dependency ratio, supervision, and the borrower's perception of repayment possess statistically significant explanatory power regarding the likelihood of loan diversion to non-productive investments, relative to the absence of such diversion, assuming *ceteris paribus*. The likelihood of not diverting the loan, in relation to the base category, is significantly influenced by the borrower's sex, group size, the number of females in the group, and perceptions regarding repayment. Given the findings, it is advisable to prioritize these significant variables to ensure the judicious use of limited resources and to formulate policies that can effectively enhance the livelihoods of small-scale borrowers.

Other variables, such as consumer and investor behaviour, market trends, the borrower's capacity for repayment of the loan, and the wealth of the household, are a few of the exogenous factors that may have an effect on the overall spending patterns of the households.

5.4.7 Outstanding loans

This analysis focuses on the outstanding loans obtained from 2 distinct lending agencies by 100 borrowers. Table 5.14 illustrates the default rates in loan repayment among 50 borrowers from each MFI. All 50 borrowers

Table 5.14 Loan outstanding (₹ in lakhs)

Institution	No. of borrowers	Loan taken	Rate of interest	Repayment due	Percentage
Bank	50	5.55	14.60%	3.20	57.66
MFI	50	4.79	14.00%	4.71	98.43
Total	**100**	**10.34**		**7.91**	**76.55**

Source: Compiled by the author.

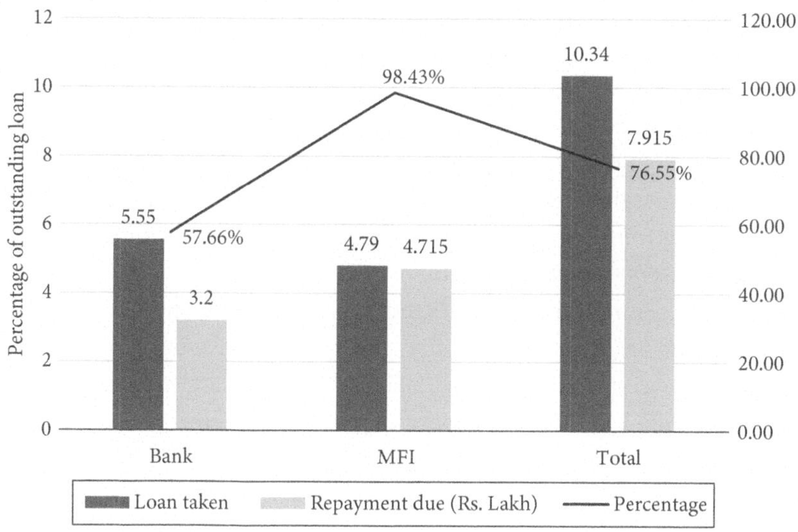

Fig. 5.14 Repayment overdue
Source: Prepared by the author.

from Bank 1 defaulted on repayments totalling ₹3.20 lakh, representing 57.66% of the loans taken, while the 50 women borrowers from the MFI defaulted by ₹4.79 lakh, accounting for 98.43%. The total outstanding loan for all 100 borrowers from both institutions was ₹7.91 lakh, compared to a loan amount of ₹10.34 lakh, representing 76.55% (Fig. 5.14).

The banks' overall NPA status may significantly diverge from the loan outstanding figures presented in this study. The total NPAs recorded by institutions at the corporate level vary due to the influence of new and consistently repaid loans, which overshadow the outstanding and problematic loans in the microcredit accounts of BLP borrowers.

5.4.8 Reasons for loan being overdue

Numerous justifications have been identified for borrowers' failure to repay loans, including those from bank branches and those from state government-operated MFIs (Fig. 5.15). The reasons articulated by the borrowers, as well as those observed, merit attention and can be enumerated as follows:

a) Design of the loan products: the author has identified a flawed loan design. When designing a loan product, it is essential to consider the borrowers' income levels, geographical location, repayment capacity, and the potential income generated from the proposed economic activity. No considerations seem to have been made in the design of the loan product. BLP individuals necessitate grants to elevate their status above the poverty threshold rather than receiving minimal loans. The socio-economic circumstances of the borrowers were disregarded.
b) Social commitments of the borrowers: social obligations, emotions, income brackets, duties, attire, and customs have been completely disregarded. Individuals with limited income are neither prohibited nor excluded from society. Regardless of their economic status,

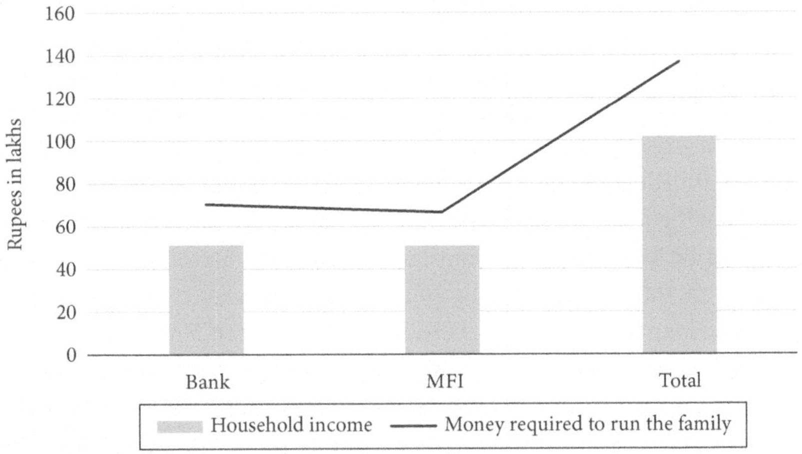

Fig. 5.15 Household income and family requirement
Source: Prepared by the author.

individuals adhere to their customs, faith, traditions, and beliefs. When individuals possess financial resources, the immediate necessity for expenditure takes precedence over investing in business and awaiting profits to fulfil their social, cultural, religious, consumption, and health requirements.

The author has determined that borrowers prioritize their customary, social, and traditional needs over investing in small economic activities, the returns of which are not assured in trade.

c) Expectation of writing off loans: numerous borrowers anticipate that the government will forgive the loans as part of its assistance to BPL families. Some local politicians also advocate for borrowers to refrain from repaying their loans. Furthermore, the financial status of the borrowers incentivizes them to decide against repaying the loans.
d) Poverty levels of borrowers: all interviewed borrowers belonged to BPL families and were individuals of limited means with inadequate income for sustenance. Consequently, they may have been unable to fully participate in economic activities while experiencing hunger.
e) Mushrooming big businesses, technological changes, and business growth: the expansion of commercial operations by large corporations, coupled with the production of affordable goods and their distribution to rural areas by major industrial firms, corporate entities, and marketing agencies, has rendered small businesses obsolete. Individuals pursuing techno-cultural transformations are disinclined to engage in commerce with small and micro vendors as well as small retail establishments. The migrant population from distant states such as Uttar Pradesh, Bihar, and Rajasthan are establishing businesses in rural and remote areas of Telangana, significantly investing, and rendering small enterprises (including vegetable vending and street vendors) obsolete.
f) Three main factors: three primary factors influence borrowers' repayment behaviour. The loan product is not viable. The minimal amount, roughly equivalent to one month's family consumption of the borrower, fails to generate sufficient income to repay the loan, sustain the family, and reinvest in the same enterprise. For instance, ₹10,000 cannot yield ₹22,000 within a month to cover the loan

instalment, sustain the family with ₹10,000, and reinvest ₹10,000 in the business. The borrowers lack personal viability. They possess their own familial and additional social obligations to fulfil. Family obligations, health issues, education, marriages, deaths, births, and similar commitments impede the borrower's ability to invest funds. The economy is insufficiently robust to absorb minor inflows and generate income from their investments.

All the aforementioned factors contribute to the overdue loans from microcredit borrowers, with social and unintended expenditures taking precedence.

5.5 Lender perception about borrowers' diversion of loans

The lenders' perception of the borrower's misappropriation of loans provides critical insights into borrowers' tendencies to divert funds for unintended purposes. Table 5.12 elucidates the perspectives of MFIs regarding the borrower. Lenders firmly assert that the loans are allocated for the alleviation of poverty among BPL families. However, they lack a response concerning how they anticipate that BPL families will invest capital in enterprises and generate sustainable income to repay the loan, fulfil familial obligations, and reinvest in the business. The lenders recognize that borrowers face greater responsibilities and obligations than merely engaging in business activities, which may lead them to allocate the loan funds to unforeseen immediate needs.

The lenders anticipate an enhancement in the borrowers' quality of life following the disbursement of the loan, provided it is utilized as intended or according to the designed loan product. Nevertheless, they have not observed any significant improvement in the quality of life of a borrower, despite urging them to utilize the loan for its intended purpose.

Lenders believe that microcredit alone is insufficient to tackle the challenges of poverty alleviation. Alternative methodologies are required. First, lenders strongly advocate that the creation of employment opportunities is preferable to providing small loans in a competitive environment dominated by mechanized production processes and large corporations. Second, the socio-economic needs of borrowers must be identified and addressed prior to soliciting their investment in minimal amounts.

5.6 MFI impact: Socio-economic reach and credit utilization

The author finds from a report published by Sa-Dhan on an impact assessment study of clients of MFIs conducted in 17 states of India during 2022–23 that 46% of microfinance loans are provided to families having monthly income less than ₹20,000, that is, servicing the population living in distress. Further, 52% of loan utilization is for working capital for their income-generating activities and 31% of loan utilization is for income-generating assets, including livestock. The first cycle of loan is used mostly for starting new enterprises, and subsequent loans cycles are for working capital requirement. Dependence on moneylenders reduced substantially (i.e. from 20.1% to 8.3%) and brought deprived populations under the institutional fold with gradual economic improvement (NABARD 2022–23). According to this report, if not explicitly documented, only 31% of the loan was allocated for working capital and income generation, while 69% was used for unintended purposes (Table 5.15).

5.7 Theory or assumption analysis

The author has developed the following three assumptions. These will be evaluated in accordance with prior research analysis and findings. To enhance reader convenience, each assumption is analysed sequentially in a continuous format, without prior enumeration, followed by separate analysis.

A1) Microcredit is not utilized by the borrowers for its intended purpose but diverted to an unintended purpose by the borrowers. The evidence unequivocally demonstrates that the borrowers have misappropriated the loans designated for microeconomic activities for personal and unintended purposes unrelated to economic endeavours. Their social obligations, traditions, societal

Table 5.15 Lender perception of loans and borrowers' economic and social status

Question	Institution One (BBPSB)	Institution Two (SRMFI)	Constructs	Measurements
What are the activities of your institution?	Banking	Microfinance	Activities of the lender	Banking and activities of microfinance—micro-saving and microcredit (micro-investment)
Do you lend for business activities by the poorest of the poor?	Yes	Yes, mostly women	Willingness to lend to the poorest of the poor	Ability to lend to the poorest of the poor
What are the activities you regularly lend to micro activities?	Any micro activity, such as street vendors, ironing, vegetables, caste-related activities, fruit sellers, homemade snacks, small Kirana shops, plumbers, electricians—or any activity that can generate income for the borrower	Any micro activity, such as street vendors, ironing, vegetables, caste-related activities, fruit sellers, homemade snacks, small Kirana shops, plumbers, electricians—or any activity that can generate income for the borrower	Regularity in lending to microbusiness activities	Spread of micro-lending across various microbusiness activities
What are the minimum and maximum amounts you lend?	Minimum ₹1,000 and maximum for micro activities up to ₹100,000, depending on the activity; however, we have given only up to ₹25,000, keeping in view the repaying capacity of the borrower and their economic behaviour	Minimum ₹1,000 and maximum for micro activities up to ₹100,000, depending on the activity; however, we have given only up to ₹25,000, keeping in view the repaying capacity of the borrower and their economic behaviour	Limitations in lending to microbusinesses	Sufficiency of limits
Do you take any security for the loan given?	No	No	Loans are not secured	Impact of unsecured loans on repayment

What is the intended purpose of the microloan you give to the borrower?	To reduce poverty by utilizing the loan in the business, generating income, supporting the family, repaying the loan, and re-investing the income over expenditure in the business to maintain the cycle	To reduce poverty by utilizing the loan in the business, generating income, supporting the family, repaying the loan, and re-investing the income over expenditure in the business to maintain the cycle	The intentions of the loan are clear to the lender, and accordingly, the loans are given	Percentage of loans used for the intended purpose
How do you identify a borrower?	Almost all of the borrowers examined are walk-in customers	We have field officers who regularly visit the target geographical locations to identify the borrowers; also, we have walk in borrowers	The lender knows to identify the prospective borrower	To what extent is the lender's knowledge put into use to identify the borrower?
Do you think that all of the borrowers are spending the amount on the intended purpose?	No	Not all	The lender is aware of the behaviour of the borrower to invest the borrowed money in the intended activity	Factual situation in relation to the lender's awareness
What is the percentage of borrowers not utilizing the amount for the intended purpose?	Only 92–98%	85–90%	Lender's awareness on percentage of utilization	Actual percentage
Do you initiate any action against the persons who do not use the money as intended?	No	No	Action against the recalcitrant borrower is available	Impact of the action if taken, null if not taken, or consequences of non-taking of action

(*continued*)

Table 5.15 Continued

Question	Institution One (BBPSB)	Institution Two (SRMFI)	Constructs	Measurements
How is the repayment behaviour of the borrowers?	Poor	Satisfactory	Unable to repay the loan	Extent of inability
What changes in quality of life do you see in the borrowers?	We have not seen any marked change in the quality of life, but the observations are that many of them are not borrowing from unregulated money lenders anymore	We have not seen any marked change in the quality of life, but the observations are that many of them are not borrowing from unregulated money lenders anymore	Change in the quality of life of the borrower should be visible	Extent of change in the quality of life
Do you think the microcredit can address the challenges of poverty reduction?	To a certain extent; microcredit alone cannot address the challenges of poverty reduction—other approaches are needed	To certain extent; microcredit alone cannot address the challenges of poverty reduction—other approaches are needed	Awareness of the lender about the microcredit intervention to poverty reduction	Level of understanding of the lender
If not, what remedial measures do you recommend?	First, we strongly recommend that the creation of employment opportunities is better than granting loans in small quantities in this competitive world, where every production process and business is mechanized and run by big corporate houses; second, socio-economic needs of the borrowers should be identified and addressed before asking them to invest and earn on tiny amounts	First, we strongly recommend that the creation of employment opportunities is better than granting loans in small quantities in this competitive world, where every production process and business is mechanized and run by big corporate houses; second, socio-economic needs of the borrowers should be identified and addressed before asking them to invest and earn on tiny amounts	Lenders can suggest remedial measures in the microcredit policy	Width of policy recommendations

Do you extend any loan for consumption purposes other than microcredit?	Yes, based on the repaying capacity of the borrower	Yes	Consumption loans are available to the borrowers	Impact of consumption loans on borrowers/ business activities
Do you have any annual targets to extend credit support to the needy?	No	No	Annual targets should be available	Extent of targets
If repayment of the loan does not come on time, do you enforce law to recover the amount?	No	No	Law enforcement mechanism is the tool to recover the loan	Extent of use of law enforcement by the lender
Do you grant a second loan if the borrower clears the first loan on time?	Yes	Yes	The second-time loans are available for the borrowers with acceptable repayment behaviour	Extent of utility of the facility

Source: Prepared by the author.

pressures, religious convictions, poverty, and political pledges have necessitated the diversion of funds to unintended purposes.

A2) There is no policy in India to address the financial requirements of the borrowers to meet their social, religious, cultural, consumption, and customary needs. The author has not identified any existing national policy framework that provides loans exclusively for the personal needs of borrowers to fulfil their traditional, social, religious, and cultural obligations. The consumption loans currently offered in conjunction with the microcredit were not linked to the social, cultural, religious, and customary obligations and needs assessment and were insufficient for the destitute applicants. Comprehensive policies are essential to develop loan products for BPL families, promoting investment, profit production, loan payback, preservation of dignity, and improvement of quality of life. Offering larger loans and investment instruction will be more advantageous than simply allocating monies to impoverished individuals.

A3) The microcredit offered by the institutions is not adequate either to meet business needs or to meet social needs. No evidence contradicts this. The collected and analysed data reveals that the insufficient loans offered by MFIs are inadequate for borrowers to initiate business endeavours, produce profits, repay the loans, meet social and family duties, and reinvest in their enterprises. The resources are insufficient to meet all social responsibilities.

Consequently, the assumptions have been validated, and the research objectives have been achieved.

6
The Way Forward

6.1 Introduction

Upon completing the study in the preceding chapters, analysing the collected data, and validating the assumption, it is time to conclude the analysis by deriving conclusions from the study and offering recommendations to enhance microcredit delivery in the country through appropriate targeting and necessary policy decisions.

6.2 The progress so far

Microfinance institutions undeniably play a pivotal role in poverty alleviation by catering to urban residents; rural smallholder farmers; small business operators; and women engaged in small trades, agricultural, and traditional caste-based activities, who are neglected by the conventional banking system, by providing financial services that fulfil the unmet demand for start-up and working capital in small quantity. Authors like Milford Bateman maintain that focusing on microfinance undermines other more significant poverty alleviation approaches such as provision of basic services like health and education (Bateman and Chang 2012). Nevertheless, borrowers may divert the loan for unintended purposes, which undermines the financial sustainability of the institutions and alters the livelihoods of the borrowers. From the analysis observations in the previous chapters, the following conclusions can be made.

6.2.1 The study indicated that out of the total sample households, 80 (80%) had diverted funds to the extent of 50.72% of for unintended purposes, while the remaining 20 (20%) had not diverted their loan to unintended goals. None of these have

Microcredit Misallocation? P. Gargi Rao, Oxford University Press. © P. Gargi Rao 2026.
DOI: 10.1093/9780197910573.003.0006

redirected the loan towards any productive endeavour. The diversions were undertaken to fulfil their social obligations. The findings demonstrate that the loan's purpose, dependency ratio, supervision, and the borrower's perception of repayment possess statistically significant explanatory power regarding the likelihood of loan diversion to non-productive investments, relative to the absence of such diversion, assuming *ceteris paribus*. The likelihood of not diverting the loan, in relation to the base category, is significantly influenced by the borrower's sex, group size, the number of females in the group, and perceptions regarding repayment. Based on the findings, it is prudent to prioritize these critical variables to ensuring efficient allocation of limited resources and to develop suitable policies that can effectively improve the livelihoods of small-scale borrowers.

6.2.2 The bankers and microfinance organizations are aware of borrowers' loan diversion, particularly observing that bankers are convinced such diversion occurs when the borrower is from a below-the-poverty-line (BPL) family. However, the loans are granted with the requirement to comply with directives from their headquarters to finance the priority sector, particularly focusing on lending to BPL families, which is central to both the priority sector and the national agenda, as stated by the microfinance institutions (MFIs).

6.2.3 The study and interviews with the borrowers explain that the borrowers are under considerable pressure from familial commitments, traditional customs, and customary limits. Situated at the bottom of the social hierarchy with restricted income, they are incapable of meeting societal expectations or efficiently leveraging the scant microcredit for business revenue growth. They face stigmatization or ostracism if they fail to engage in the social and cultural activities and obligations of their caste groups or local community. There are cases when specific borrowers used the loan monies for donations to the Ganapati Festival under coercion.

6.2.4 The study indicates that the purpose of loans, dependency ratio, oversight, and borrowers' perception of repayment substantially affect the probability of loan diversion to non-productive ventures, assuming that all other factors in the model are held constant. The borrowers' gender, group size, number of females in the group, and attitudes towards payback are statistically significant factors influencing the probability of reallocating the loan to non-productive investments as opposed to loans that remain directed towards productive uses.

6.2.5 The diversion may stem from an insufficient evaluation of borrowers' economic, social, and sustenance requirements; their poverty levels; and the market dynamics influencing microeconomic activities due to rapid technology developments affecting industry and commerce and changing consumer tastes.

6.2.6 No conclusive policies exist from either bankers or government-associated MFIs to create alternative livelihoods for BPL households, nor to incentivize micro-investors to efficiently utilize the funds designated for particular economic activity. No strategy exists that prioritizes the evaluation of borrowers' personal viability before encouraging them to acquire modest loans for investment, profit production, and loan payback. No assessment appears to have been made to measure the impact on micro enterprises of the cheap consumer durables imported. No policy recognizes the social, customary, and traditional requirements of borrowers or addresses these issues, particularly among BPL families.

6.2.7 No evidence demonstrates that the borrowers' quality of living increased after acquiring loans for microcredit operations. All borrowers, irrespective of their classification as BPL families, own a mobile phone, a gas cooker, and a small television in their residences. However, motorbikes, refrigerators, geysers, washing machines, kitchen grinders, and other appliances are lacking among all debtors. No evidence demonstrates that the borrowers' quality of living increased after acquiring loans for microcredit operations. With the exception of 7 out of 100 interviewers, none has their own residential unit. Several individuals have submitted applications for a double-bedroomed house promised by the Telangana state government. Several individuals, seeking anonymity, stated they are employed as manual labourers or in other small enterprises as daily and monthly wage earners, despite having acquired microcredit.

6.2.8 Some borrowers either obtained funds from alternative sources alongside the loan, liquidated ancestral property, or sold small amounts of gold for their daughters' marriages, family health, celebrating festivals, shraddha ceremonies, childbirth, and their children's education.

6.2.9 While the examination of self-help groups (SHGs) is not included in this study, informal discussions with borrowers indicated that SHG members are in a more advantageous position as the SHG is accountable to the MFI rather than the individual. Furthermore, SHGs primarily provide loans for the personal expenditure of the borrowers, and there is no strict requirement for borrowers to invest solely in designated economic activities. Consequently, the members of SHGs procure loans from the SHG, allocate the funds for their social necessities, and repay the loans using their income derived from casual and agricultural labour.

6.2.10 The unequivocal conclusion is that microcredit is misallocated and diverted from its intended purpose. Borrowers, despite understanding that such diversion contravenes the regulations of MFIs, redirect the loans to meet the demands of bank interest rates, as well as cultural, social, traditional, and customary obligations, and lenders knowingly ignore such diversion in some cases, where the repayment is timely.

6.2.11 The study records that the non-performing assets (NPAs) of banks have been increasing annually, while the NPAs of non-banking financial companies (NBFCs) has been decreasing over the years. This clearly demonstrates that private-sector NBFCs prioritize profit and business objectives, while public-sector banks emphasize social responsibilities related to poverty alleviation for their target borrowers. The NPAs of not-for-profit (NFP) MFIs have shown an increasing trend, indicating that borrowers involved in micro activities are inadequately generating revenue to repay loans from financial institutions; rather, the funds have been misappropriated for unintended uses instead of income generation. The decrease in NPAs among NBFCs does not indicate that the borrower has effectively generated income to service the loan. The rigorous recovery protocols enacted by the NBFCs, along with the recovery strategies articulated by specific borrowers during site visits, are sometimes regarded as inhumane; thus, assets are liquidated to settle debts to maintain social standing.

6.2.12 The study indicates that microcredit has failed to yield the anticipated outcomes due to the minimal loan amounts provided; the pre-existing poverty of the target demographic; and the prevailing social, cultural, and religious commitments, practices, and beliefs influencing their lives. The research provides evidence that borrowers from microcredit institutions prefer the initiation of punitive actions by lenders over being ostracized, marginalized, or socially stigmatized for failing to meet customary obligations and social expenditures.

6.2.13 Theoretically, microfinance can enhance the financial inclusion of low-income households and contribute to the attainment of certain Sustainable Development Goals (SDGs) through multiple mechanisms. The condition are that borrowers must demonstrate personal viability prior to securing a loan from microcredit organizations, and the loan should not serve as their exclusive means of sustenance.

6.2.14 As discussed earlier, microfinance refers to the delivery of financial services (such as loans (microcredit), savings, insurance, and money transfer services) to individuals and small enterprises lacking access to conventional banking. Microfinance encompasses several modalities, such as group-based lending (SHGs), individual lending, savings-led financing, and microinsurance. Microfinance is an effective instrument for combating poverty, fostering entrepreneurship, and facilitating economic development.

6.2.15 These services are generally offered by MFIs, which focus on assisting low-income and financially marginalized communities. The objective of microfinance is to enable individuals and small businesses to initiate or grow their ventures, enhance their living standards, and augment their economic prospects.

6.2.16 Evaluated in light of these objectives, microcredit in this work has demonstrated contrary results. Microcredit can assist borrowers in achieving their objectives only when their small business or economic activity suffers from a lack of capital, but the borrowers from BPL families themselves are financially strained and compelled to spend on social events beyond their means. The society they are living in demands that the individuals first meet their social obligations. Therefore, the borrower prioritizes spending on social events first rather than investing and earning profits.

6.2.17 Microfinance facilitates the achievement of the SDGs by granting access to financial services for marginalized populations, including low-income individuals and small enterprises. This can mitigate poverty and foster economic development and growth, which are essential elements of various SDGs, including SDG 1 (No poverty), SDG 8 (Decent work and economic growth), and SDG 9 (Industry, innovation, and infrastructure). Nevertheless, nearly all borrowers interviewed for the study have clearly not generated any income from the borrowed funds and have instead allocated the loan towards social expenditures. This indicates that microcredit adversely affects borrowers when their subsistence needs (including social obligations) are not considered in the loan amount, or when microcredit is exclusively provided to individuals already operating businesses and suffering from capital shortages. The absence of help poses a risk of their descent into poverty. Consequently, microcredit will tackle contingent poverty but not sustenance poor.

6.2.18 Microcredit can additionally advance other SDGs, including SDG 2 (Zero hunger) by facilitating credit access for small farmers and food producers, and SDG 5 (Gender equality) by offering financial services to women who might otherwise be marginalized from the official financial system.

6.2.19 Ultimately, microcredit and microfinancial services are not intended for impoverished populations burdened by poverty and social obligations, notwithstanding their distressing circumstances. The financial hardship of births and deaths in BPL households is equivalent. States should not encourage them to engage in transactions involving modest sums to generate revenue for the lending institution because at the end of the day, it is the financing institution that earns profit from microcredit, not the borrower.

6.3 Summary of the conclusions

6.3.1 Microcredit, an initiative designed to empower the impoverished, has frequently faced substantial and intricate challenges in implementation. Although these loans are intended to initiate small, income-generating ventures, borrowers frequently encounter significant societal pressure that can redirect the cash to non-business expenditures. Within the designated borrower cohort, a household's status is contingent upon its capacity to organize social gatherings such as festivals, weddings, births, and funerals. This expectation compels borrowers to allocate a segment of their loan for these rituals to uphold their reputation and evade social ostracism, a choice motivated not by financial imprudence but by potent societal conventions. In certain microcredit models, the 'joint-liability' approach, wherein group members share collective responsibility for one another's loans, can exacerbate this pressure as individuals may feel compelled to participate in group activities or support fellow members with their social expenditures to maintain group cohesion.

6.3.2 The intrinsic challenge of managing household finances significantly influences the allocation of microloans. In a low-income household managing various pressing financial obligations, funds from a microloan are typically interchangeable and rapidly blend with other sources of income. It is an impractical assumption to assume that these assets may be entirely allocated for an income generation initiative when urgent necessities such as health care, education, and everyday consumption demand consideration. Confronted with the intricate and conflicting demands of daily life, borrowers sometimes utilize loans to alleviate cash flow deficiencies or meet urgent needs, despite the original intention for long-term business investments. Moreover, insufficient financial literacy, particularly among poorer families, might result in borrowers possessing inadequate financial planning abilities, hindering their capacity to manage finances effectively and prioritizing long-term productive investments over immediate, non-productive expenditures.

6.3.3 In addition to social pressures and household management difficulties, borrowers frequently encounter structural and human obstacles that hinder the loan's intended objective. Numerous individuals, despite their best intentions, encounter difficulties in utilizing the loan to effectively create income due to an absence of a suitable company strategy, pertinent skills, or market prospects. This results in the loan being allocated to alternative, unproductive purposes. The obligation to adhere to payback deadlines, occasionally exacerbated by exploitative lending practices from microfinance firms, propels borrowers into a precarious situation. To preserve their social status and secure future loans, they allocated the original monies to social activities, so establishing a debt cycle in which new loans are incurred to repay existing ones. Elevated interest rates and stringent repayment requirements can intensify this cycle, driving borrowers into over-indebtedness and further away from their initial objectives.

6.3.4 The intricate interaction of social variables, household financial conditions, and systemic obstacles undermines the simplified narrative of microcredit as a direct route to empowerment. Although designed to facilitate an escape from poverty, many borrowers confront entrenched social expectations and pressing survival necessities. The misallocation of finances signifies a calculated reaction to the complex challenges posed by poverty rather than merely a deficiency of discipline. It exposes the inadequacies of a uniform approach to financial aid and underscores the necessity for a more comprehensive understanding of the socio-economic context in which microcredit functions. The purpose of microcredit should be comprehended as a means to assist individuals in overcoming poverty rather than incurring debt.

6.4 The way forward or the road ahead

6.4.1 The findings indicate that prioritizing these critical variables is vital for the judicious use of limited resources and the development of effective policies that can improve the fortunes of BPL families and micro borrowers. The prioritization of subsidized or free food grains for BPL families, coupled with the provision of quality health care, education, transportation, and housing, should be emphasized in state policies designed to assist the impoverished prior to promoting income generation through microcredit.

6.4.2 A pressing need exists for a microcredit policy that emphasizes, recognizes, identifies, and addresses the personal requirements of borrowers before the granting of microloans for income-generating activities. The requirement for social events should be included in the loan amount allocated for each activity sponsored by MFIs.

6.4.3 It is imperative to identify BPL households and furnish them with employment chances in both the private and public sectors rather than solely offering financial help and anticipating their autonomous income generation and troubling them on non-payment of equated monthly instalment on time. The government is accountable for mitigating poverty through means other than microcredit. Individuals in extreme poverty could not allocate even minimal amounts of capital to yield returns. Employing individuals from BPL families in government-led industries and business activities, contingent upon their suitability for deployment, or providing necessary training to these individuals prior to their engagement in public activities, is a superior alternative to offering microloans.

6.4.4 It is essential to formulate and implement capacity and skill development training programmes for individuals from BPL households, facilitating their access to public and private work for immediate financial support. Only persons engaged in family businesses or caste-specific occupations, who aspire to self-employment, should be encouraged to obtain increased microcredit for suitable investment. Essential backward and forward links, encompassing start-up financing, operating capital, marketing support, and partnerships with procurement agencies, must be formed to ensure their full participation in the activity.

6.4.5 A compilation of traditional activities requiring low investment should be created and distributed for MFIs to consult before approving microcredit. The lending institution must continually monitor the credit extended to prevent misappropriations, discover diversion needs, and facilitate new loans, allowing borrowers to concentrate on their economic pursuits.

6.4.6 All microcredit borrowers should be incorporated into a government-supported national pension programme requiring modest contributions from the borrowers. All borrowers should be incorporated into the national health programme, including gratis health care in both private and public hospitals without limitations on medical expenses.

6.4.7 The government should relocate all the regional rural banks (RRBs) to rural areas from their current locations in urban and semi-urban areas. There is an urgent necessity for government-controlled rural microcredit institutions like RRBs to seriously engage themselves in poverty reduction, keeping aside their own commercial viability. RRBs, established under the RRB Act of 1976, previously provided significant assistance in alleviating rural poverty. Since the merger and the transition from rural to urban areas, RRBs have increasingly prioritized profit generation by financing large enterprises, housing, vehicles, and other financially viable loans to institutions. If relocating RRBs to rural areas is unfeasible, a new public-sector banking system specifically for rural microfinance should be instituted. Private financial institutions that extend credit secured by gold, real estate, or residential properties to families in rural and urban regions have emerged, characterized by exorbitant interest rates and stringent recovery practices. Nevertheless, individuals procure loans from these institutions solely to fulfil urgent requirements and evade social obligations.

6.4.8 The author firmly believes that microcredit fails to fulfil its intended objectives of alleviating poverty, enhancing quality of life, and empowering women economically. The programmes such as Swarna Jayanti Gram Swarozgar Yojna (Mission for Elimination of Urban Poverty) have also not shown the desired results; in many cases, the assets have been diverted to pressing social expenditure by the borrowers. It is recommended that the aforementioned policy changes be implemented promptly following extensive discussions among stakeholders and experts.

6.4.9 The government must acknowledge that the microcredit approach to poverty reduction is introduced on the shortcomings of the formal financial sector. It is imperative to maintain focus on the vision of financial inclusion for all citizens of India. The foundational concept of microfinance is profoundly significant; it provides financial inclusion opportunities to individuals who might otherwise lack access. As microfinance progresses, it is crucial to continually assess its effectiveness and determine whether it represents the optimal allocation of resources. If the private sector perceives all government intervention as an impediment, addressing deficiencies within the sector will become significantly more challenging. The government can promote ethical practices and impose penalties for misconduct; however, in a sector with millions of clients and transactions in relatively isolated regions, complete oversight is unattainable. Private MFIs must assume the responsibility for the consequences of their actions as microfinance transcends mere profit generation and is integral to a wider initiative for poverty alleviation.

6.4.10 Microcredit is defined by the Investopedia as follows: 'Microfinance, also called microcredit, is a type of banking service provided to low-income individuals or groups who otherwise wouldn't have access to financial services' (Investopedia 2024). It is therefore the credit given to the low-income individuals or groups who otherwise would not have access to financial services. Currently, access to financial services is available to anybody possessing investable money, whether for business ventures or banking deposits. Individuals living in BPL situations are excluded from financial services because they do not possess investible money.

6.4.11 Even if financial institutions attempt to improve accessibility, they are unlikely to offer services as the likelihood of repayment from the borrower of the BPL family is minimal. Individuals below the poverty level are unlikely to seek loans honestly to make an investment and generate income, which is not possible for them under the conditions already discussed.

6.4.12 The borrower from the BPL family looks first at subsistence needs, family responsibilities, and then social needs. If all these are met from the loan taken, then the borrower will attempt to invest to generate income, repay the loan, meet family needs, and re-invest consequently. It is extremely hard for individuals from BPL families to secure microcredit and escape poverty. Only employment, subsidized food, health care, shelter, education, and social assistance in old age will address the challenges faced by the poor.

6.5 Summing up

Policymakers must first acknowledge that microcredit, when minimally allocated to illiterate BPL individuals, cannot yield three sustainable sources of income: one for loan repayment through equated monthly instalments, a second for family expenses, and a third for reinvestment in the business to sustain the operational cycle.

Microcredit, defined as small-scale lending to impoverished individuals, is incorporated into a dynamic macroeconomic model of income distribution. People out of formal employment and the poor select from three occupational alternatives: subsistence production, small-scale project investment, and large-scale project investment. Subsistence activities are devoid of costs and risks, but project investments are characterized by the contrary and may necessitate external financing. Financial firms have deficient contract enforcement capabilities. Without microcredit, only substantial, collateralized loans are accessible via the conventional banking sector. In these conditions, early disparities endure as only the affluent can secure these loans, while small-scale and micro enterprises are either unviable or unprofitable. The advent of microcredit renders this endeavour feasible and appealing by offering non-collateralized loans and additional characteristics of microlending agreements. Policymakers and microcredit practitioners felt that the microcredit instruments could reduce poverty if the benefit extended to the BPL cohort. The outcome is expected to be a reduction in poverty and inequality.

Disproving the above expectation, this study elucidates the prevalence of microloan diversion by the borrowers from BPL families, utilizing data from a primary household survey. Loan diversion is a complex socio-economic phenomenon since its origins may be found in societal structures and norms or may stem from legitimate economic necessities. In circumstances where loan diversion is motivated by legitimate economic necessities such as obtaining food, medical care, or education, it serves as a replacement for the absent social security system. It serves a crucial economic function even when allocated to purposes that do not immediately enhance physical production. This work's descriptive analysis indicates that the loans are primarily diverted to satisfy social, consumption, and medical requirements. We can ascertain, at least in the situation examined, that the redirected loans fulfil a significant economic role.

The research has revealed that although formal loans impose harsher conditions, semi-formal loans are more available and subject to less oversight. Consequently, they are redirected from their intended purpose. This supports Pearlman's (2012) theoretical model, which posits that neglecting ex ante consumption smoothing in the provision of formal MFI loans will result in increased diversion of semi-formal loans.

This topic requires a dual-faceted strategy for policy matters. Individuals should be afforded a safeguard against adversity and financial assistance for enduring income loss through access to insurance for the former and social security provisions for the latter. Loans with simplified terms to address consumer, medical, or social duty requirements may serve as an alternative solution. The semi-formal loans require enhanced oversight for intended utility by the borrower and for timely recovery. A strategy designed for poverty reduction through the production of productive assets and gainful employment by providing collateral-free loans, social assistance, and other doles to the impoverished should prioritize the effective utilization of these loans rather than maximizing disbursement. To be truly effective, the two policies must operate in conjunction. Enhanced oversight of microcredit, without offering alternative, more affordable credit sources to satisfy other requirements, is certain to fail since it fails to tackle the issue of loan diversion.

This study clarifies several characteristics peculiar to the economic and social life of borrowers that may contribute to loan diversion; however, many aspects remain unexamined. First, the survey provides ex post data regarding the occurrence of loan diversion; nevertheless, it remains unclear whether this diversion is deliberate or inadvertent. The problem of inadvertent loan diversion for consumption stabilization due to abrupt income shocks can be addressed through the provision of income assistance or insurance. However, the deliberate misallocation of loans from economic uses to ostentatious expenditure carries significant socio-moral implications. A microcredit intended for the establishment of productive assets will be ineffective if misallocated to fulfil social expenditure demands arising from entrenched societal norms and customs such as dowry, feasts for funerals, childbirth, and puberty celebrations for girls.

Second, this work relies on data gathered from a specific region, thereby representing just the socio-cultural attributes of that locale. Social compulsions may vary across different locations. The proportion of sampling units that divert loans is minimal. Consequently, we may not derive any reliable predictions from this analysis. Subsequent research in additional areas would provide us with a more profound understanding of the issue of loan diversion.

Ultimately, this study possesses an additional restriction. This relates to the occurrence of loan default. The issue of loan default is an unavoidable consequence of loan diversion. Nonetheless, the current study did not elucidate this issue, which may be regarded as a prospective field for further investigation. A study that incorporates both difficulties would be more thorough and would elucidate the long-term effects of the problem on loan diversion.

ANNEXURE I

List of Non-Banking Finance Company–Microfinance Institutions Registered with the Reserve Bank of India (31 January 2022)

S. no.	Name of the company	Regional office
1	Ceejay Microfin Limited	Ahmedabad
2	Namra Finance Limited	Ahmedabad
3	Pahal Financial Services Limited	Ahmedabad
4	Prayas Financial Services Private Limited	Ahmedabad
5	Shroff Capital & Finance Private Limited	Ahmedabad
6	Avanti Microfinance Private Limited	Bengaluru
7	Chaitanya India Fin Credit Private Limited	Bengaluru
8	CreditAccess Grameen Limited	Bengaluru
9	Idf Financial Services Private Limited	Bengaluru
10	Nabfins Limited	Bengaluru
11	Navachetana Microfin Services Private Limited	Bengaluru
12	Rors Finance Private Limited	Bengaluru
13	Samasta Microfinance Limited	Bengaluru
14	Shree Marikamba Microfinance Private Limited	Bengaluru
15	South India Finvest Private Limited	Bengaluru
16	Aviral Finance Private Limited	Bhopal
17	Adhikar Microfinance Ltd (Trfd from Ahmedabad)	Bhubaneshwar
18	Annapurna Finance Private Limited	Bhubaneshwar
19	G. U. Financial Services Private Limited	Bhubaneshwar
20	Vector Finance Private Limited	Bhubaneshwar
21	Midland Microfin Limited	Chandigarh
22	Asirvad Microfinance Limited	Chennai
23	Belstar Microfinance Limited	Chennai
24	Bwda Finance Limited	Chennai
25	Growing Opportunity Finance(India) Pvt. Ltd	Chennai
26	Kiara microcredit Private Limited	Chennai

S. no.	Name of the company	Regional office
27	Madura Microfinance Limited	Chennai
28	Magalir Micro Capital Private Limited	Chennai
29	Msm Microfinance Limited	Chennai
30	Palma Development Finance Private Limited	Chennai
31	Repco Microfinance Limited	Chennai
32	S.M.I.L.E. Microfinance Limited	Chennai
33	Svasti Microfinance Pvt. Ltd	Chennai
34	Valar Aditi Social Finance Private Limited	Chennai
35	Varam Capital Private Limited	Chennai
36	Virutcham Microfinance Limited	Chennai
37	Vivardhana Microfinance Ltd	Chennai
38	Vruksha Microfin Private Limited	Chennai
39	Wesghats Microfinance Limited	Chennai
40	Ajagar Finance Private Limited	Guwahati
41	Asomi Finance Private Ltd	Guwahati
42	Grameen Development & Finance Private Limited	Guwahati
43	Nightingale Finvest Pvt. Ltd	Guwahati
44	Satra Development Finance Private Limited	Guwahati
45	Unacco Financial Services Private Limited	Guwahati
46	Yvu Financial Services Pvt. Ltd	Guwahati
47	Share Microfin Ltd	Hyderabad
48	Spandana Sphoorty Financial Ltd	Hyderabad
49	Vaya Finserve Private Limited	Hyderabad
50	Arth Microfinance (Private) Ltd	Jaipur
51	Digamber Capfin Ltd	Jaipur
52	Margdarshak Financial Services Limited	Kanpur
53	Samavesh Finserve Private Limited	Kanpur
54	Sindhuja microcredit Private Limited	Kanpur
55	Sonata Finance Private Limited	Kanpur
56	Arohan Financial Services Limited	Kolkata
57	Asa International India Microfinance Limited	Kolkata
58	Destiny Finco (P.) Ltd	Kolkata
59	Grameen Shakti Microfinance Services Private Limited	Kolkata
60	Jagaran Microfin Private Limited (SBT Consultants (P) Ltd)	Kolkata
61	Janakalyan Financial Services Private Limited	Kolkata
62	Sarala Development & Microfinance Private Limited	Kolkata
63	Sarwadi Finance Private Limited	Kolkata
64	Uttrayan Financial Services Private Limited	Kolkata

S. no.	Name of the company	Regional office
65	Vedika Credit Capital Limited	Kolkata
66	Village Financial Services Limited	Kolkata
67	Agora Microfinance India Ltd	Mumbai
68	Anik Financial Services Pvt. Ltd	Mumbai
69	Blue Horizon Investments Limited	Mumbai
70	Centrum Microcredit Limited (Centrum Microcredit Private Limited)	Mumbai
71	Fino Finance Pvt. Limited	Mumbai
72	Hindusthan Microfinance Pvt. Ltd—MFI	Mumbai
73	Inditrade Microfinance Limited	Mumbai
74	M. Power Microfinance Pvt. Ltd	Mumbai
75	Muthoot Microfin Ltd (as Panchratna Securities Limited)—MFI	Mumbai
76	Pujan Investment & Finance Private Limited	Mumbai
77	Sahayog Microfinance Limited	Mumbai
78	Svamaan Financial Services Private Limited	Mumbai
79	Svatantra Microfin Private Limited	Mumbai
80	Unnati Microfin Private Limited (Shree Om Credit Co. Pvt. Ltd)	Mumbai
81	Altura Financial Services Limited	New Delhi
82	Capital Trust Microfinance Private Limited	New Delhi
83	Fusion Microfinance Limited	New Delhi
84	Humana Financial Services Private Limited	New Delhi
85	Light Microfinance Private Limited	New Delhi
86	Magenta Finance Services Private Limited	New Delhi
87	Mitrata Inclusive Financial Services Pvt. Ltd	New Delhi
88	Need Livelihood Microfinance Privat Limited	New Delhi
89	Prayatna Microfinance Limited	New Delhi
90	S. V. Creditline Limited	New Delhi
91	Saija Finance Private Limited	New Delhi
92	Satin Creditcare Network Limited	New Delhi
93	Satya Microcapital Limited	New Delhi
94	Save Microfinance Private Limited	New Delhi
95	Shikhar Microfinance Private Limited	New Delhi
96	Adi Chitragupta Finance Limited	Patna
97	Janashree Microfin Limited	Thiruvananthapuram

Source: RBI and National Bank for Agriculture and Rural Development (NABARD) public documents.

ANNEXURE II

Weaker Section Lending by Regional Rural Banks (National Bank for Agriculture and Rural Development) (31 March 2022)

S. no.	Name of regional rural bank (RRB)	Of total loans o/s, loans to weaker sections under priority sector		Of total loans o/s, loans to small and marginal farmers	
		No. of a/cs	Amount	No. of a/cs	Amount
1	Andhra Pragathi GB	890,469	1,135,443.79	723,025	1,021,599.39
2	Chaitany a Godavari GB	510,667	610,139.06	404,015	382,546.55
3	Saptagiri GB	401,038	556,056.78	349,730	476,561.97
4	Arunachal Pradesh RB	4,623	4,096.95	4,623	4,096.95
5	Assam GVB	471,466	311,711.12	291,697	164,874.34
6	Dakshin Bihar GB	811,328	730,167.00	735,432	698,001.00
7	Uttar Bihar GB	1,289,886	807,729.00	1,173,360	701,010.36
8	Chhattisgarh RGB	182,444	159,942.67	111,126	68,181.13
9	Baroda Gujarat GB	185,729	239,981.36	158,188	200,268.63
10	Saurashtra GB	131,139	169,676.50	123,207	154,470.79
11	Sarva Haryana GB	326,823	634,588.14	288,683	596,237.60
12	Himachal Pradesh GB	77,562	165,525.00	83,366	128,152.00
13	Ellaquai Dehati Bank	23,608	31,369.14	24,805	24,797.69
14	J & K GB	111,484	92,457.27	91,472	64,717.68
15	Jharkhand RGB	442,999	287,263.49	442,999	287,263.49
16	Karnataka GB	1,288,050	1,587,995.16	1,047,106	1,201,869.10
17	Karnataka Vikas GB	384,113	596,928.50	327,892	356,186.81
18	Kerala GB	1,255,739	1,476,655.56	917,374	985,289.81
19	Madhya Pradesh GB	485,095	544,362.37	196,945	272,588.70
20	Madhy Anchal GB	195,453	144,709.00	107,206	53,709.08
21	Maharashtra GB	376,528	281,464.34	358,542	260,963.72

(*continued*)

S. no.	Name of regional rural bank (RRB)	Of total loans o/s, loans to weaker sections under priority sector		Of total loans o/s, loans to small and marginal farmers	
		No. of a/cs	Amount	No. of a/cs	Amount
22	Vidharbha Konkan GB	183,850	183,736.63	125,757	107,305.01
23	Manipur RB	17,641	1,0102.19	15,406	8,841.85
24	Meghalaya RB	49,193	55,409.37	35,369	19,209.01
25	Mizoram RB	35,167	49,770.03	32,280	46,125.95
26	Nagaland RB	2,546	2,364.55	1,034	928.44
27	Odisha GB	507,317	367,724.60	279,649	195,099.45
28	Utkal GB	211,466	173,384.00	239,748	153,243.71
29	Puduvai Bharathiyar B	73,298	53,289.74	60,188	48,164.16
30	Punjab GB	262,652	506,846.42	215,988	472,180.85
31	Baroda Rajasthan KGB	507,544	1,132,550.75	450,271	788,705.39
32	Rajasthan Marudhara GB	144,253	274,679.69	138,740	273,136.53
33	Tamil Nadu GB	1,115,887	1,020,814.08	1,079,946	959,317.71
34	Andhra Pradesh GVB	1,319,978	1,675,793.70	1,086,195	1,351,499.71
35	Telangana GB	525,523	674,774.81	523,402	618,239.34
36	Tripura GB	222,416	185,205.78	134,905	39,817.73
37	Aryavart Bank	1,380,733	1,511,190.44	1,226,796	1.461,141.25
38	Barida U.P. Bank	1,290,544	1,348,209.01	935,177	984,094.17
39	Prathama U.P. GB	735,921	1,144,516.00	760,276	1,137,345.00
40	Uttarakhand GB	64,184	58,375.62	51,332	29,683.56
41	Bangiya GVB	513,974	443,499.00	488,314	398,254.00
42	Paschim Banga GB	158,221	235,242.08	118,302	157,848.60
43	Uttar Banga KGB	136,408	186,084.57	114,869	156,702.79
All-India total		**19,304,959**	**21,861,825.26**	**16,074,737**	**17,510,271.00**

Source: NABARD annual report on the performance of RRBs.

ANNEXURE III

Microloan
Meaning, Benefits, and How to Apply

A microloan, also referred to as a microfinance loan, is a small loan offered by authorized financial institutions to low-income households and small enterprises of India. Such loans are collateral-free and can be used for both business and household consumption to meet an end purpose. Such loans are also provided to members of self-help groups (SHGs) or joint-liability groups (JLGs) under the group lending guidelines of the bank. This data pertains to microloans provided by major public, private, and small finance banks and lists a top offering to suit borrowers' funding needs.

Policy name	Loan amount	Interest rate (min., avg., max.)	Assignees
Bank of India	Up to ₹50,000	13.10% | 13.60% | 14.10%	Individual households
ICICI Bank	NA	15% | 21.50% | 26%	MFIs, JLGs
HDFC Bank	₹15,000–₹1 lakh	15–19% (SHGs) | 22–25% (JLGs)	SHGs and JLGs
Axis Bank	₹12,000–I₹80,000	24–24.5%	MFIs, JLGs, SHGs
IndusInd Bank	NA	20.25% | 24.70%	Individual households, SHGs, JLGs
DCB Bank	Up to ₹2 lakh	24–26%	Individual households and JLGs
Suryoday Small Finance Bank	Up to 50,000 (JLGs) | ₹1.5 lakh (households)	23.35–28%	JLGs, individual households
Ujjivan Small Finance Bank	₹5,000–₹1 lakh	22% (JLGs) | 23.25–24% (households)	JLGs, individual households
Equitas Small Finance Bank	Up to ₹60,000	18% | 23% | 26%	BCs
State Bank of India		12.15%	SHG
Regional rural banks	Up to ₹100,000	11.5% | 15% | 20%	SHG

Source: Adapted from Dipen Pradhan, 'Forbes: Best Microloans of 2023: Meaning, Features & How to Apply', 28 July 2023.

Features and benefits of microloans

The Reserve Bank of India (RBI) has given approval to offer microfinance loans to commercial banks, cooperative banks, and microfinance institutions (MFIs), non-banking financial company-led MFIs (NBFC–MFIs), and housing finance companies (excluding payments banks).

The microloan can be as low as ₹5,000, with the maximum amount not exceeding 50% of the household's annual income of ₹3 lakh. Such loans are provided to households (a family of husband, wife, and children) whose aggregate annual income does not exceed ₹3 lakh. Popularly, authorized financial institutions provide such loans to SHGs or JLGs under the group lending guidelines of the bank. The interest rates are applied on microloans when the equated monthly instalment (EMI) begins. The loan amount is dispersed within the same day or might take weeks, depending upon the submission of documents and proof of income.

The RBI implemented a fair practice code for microfinance loans on 1 April 2022. Some of the major features of microloans provided by scheduled banks include the following:

Eligibility

Individual borrowers: lending institutions provide individuals (18–65 years of age) or households (families of husband, wife, and children) with microfinance loans whose annual income after adding the amount of any existing loan altogether does not exceed ₹3 lakh per annum or does not fall under the country's income tax slabs.

SHGs: banks also provide microfinance loans to SHGs, comprising individuals or entrepreneurs, to help them meet their credit needs. Usually, lending institutions partner with self-help group promoting institutions (SHPIs) and non-governmental organizations (NGOs) to facilitate microloans to socially and economically backward households.

JLGs: lending institutions also have a partnership agreement with NBFC–MFIs, who act as business correspondents to offer microfinance loans to low-income households. In the JLG group-lending model, each member takes the liability for the loans taken by other members. In such lending, borrowers are not relieved from their obligations until the time that the loan amount is repaid in full.

Maximum loan amount

Microfinance lenders usually provide loans up to ₹1 lakh or above if the principal and the interest rate amount of the borrowed sum do not exceed a limit of a maximum of 50% of the household's monthly income (adding the amount of any existing loan) of ₹3 lakh.

Loan tenure

- Individual lenders: up to 36 months
- SHGs/limited-liability loans (LLGs): 12–24 months

Margin requirement

Nil.

Processing fee

Most microfinance lenders do not charge a processing fee on loans up to ₹25,000. However, depending upon banks and the kind of borrowers (individual, JLGs, or SHGs), the processing fee can range between 1% and 3% for loans above ₹25,000.

Turn-around time (TAT)

Microfinance loans are usually dispersed within the same day of filing an application or can take weeks, depending upon the approval process of the lending institutions.

Repayment

Borrowers have to pay the EMI within a scheduled due date for the entire tenure to avoid charges. The EMI amount is collected through standing instructions given to the bank to deduct the payment on the scheduled due date from the borrowers' savings account.

In case of a failure of repayment of the overdue amount due to insufficient funds in the savings account, even after exceeding warnings from the bank, recovery agents are engaged by banks to recover dues from borrowers. Remember, non-payment of EMIs on microloans attracts overdue charges on each EMI bounce, and this will not only be hefty during payment but also dent your CIBIL score.

Prepayment or foreclosure

Microfinance loans do not have a prepayment penalty as mandated by the RBI. This means that if a borrower wishes to close the loan before the scheduled date, such loans do not carry any penalty or added interest. Depending on the lending institutions, prepayment may only be allowed after completion of a certain number of EMIs.

Charges

Microfinance lenders upload all charges on their website, and their applicability varies among banks. Some of them include

- charges applicable for delayed payment of EMIs;
- credit shield insurance charge, if opted for by borrowers;
- charges for documentation and services.

Documentation

Microloans require minimal documentation for individual microfinance borrowers, as follows:

- identity and address proof: a copy of the voter ID card, driving licence, or Aadhaar card;
- loan track records (if any loans are obtained);
- proof of income.

Interest rate

The rate of interest (RoI) on microloans differs among banks as well as borrowers, including individual households, SHGs,) and JLGs, or self-help institutions (SHIs), NGOs, and other MFIs.

Differences and similarities between microfinance and business loans

Microfinance for business consumption can be understood as a small loan given to start a business, whereas a business loan can be used to meet the working capital requirement. Some major similarities and differences between the microloan and business loan are as follows:

Microloan	Business loan
The maximum value on microloans is usually up to ₹2 lakh, or the principal and the interest rate component of the borrowed sum cannot exceed 50% of the household's monthly income.	The loan amount on business loans can be as per the requirement of the borrower.
Microloans are collateral-free.	Business loans may or may not require collateral.

Microloan	Business loan
Maximum loan tenure is up to three years.	Business loans have a maximum tenure of up to 10 years.
Microloans are disbursed as term loans.	Business loans can be term loans with overdraft and cash credit facilities.
There is no prepayment fee or requirement of margin.	Depending on banks, business loans may attract a prepayment fee and require a margin.
There is a processing fee up to 1.20%.	There is a processing fee of nil to 3.5%.
Households' income should not exceed ₹3 lakh per annum.	Business loans are disbursed as per the capital requirement of the business.
Microloans are also given through SHGs and JLGs.	Business loans are given to individual businesses alone.

Source: Adapted from Dipen Pradhan, 'Forbes: Best Microloans of 2023: Meaning, Features & How to Apply', 28 July 2023.

ANNEXURE IV

Items Included in the Borrower Behaviour Questionnaire

Section	Constructs	Measurement items
Section A: Demographical profile of the borrower	Gender	Gender of the respondent
	Age	Age of the respondent
	Marital status	Marital status of the respondent
	Educational qualification	Highest level of education obtained by the respondent
	Occupation	Occupation of the respondent
	Monthly income	Monthly income earned by the respondent
	Number of children	Children of the respondent
	School-going children	School-going children of the respondent
Section B: Basic information about the institution	Name of the institution	Name of the institution from which credit is currently drawn
	Other sources of credit available	Other sources of credit
	Amount of loan drawn	Amount of loan drawn from current institution
	Credit purpose	Purpose of taking credit by you
	Loan term	Duration of the loan granted to you
	Knowledge about the loan	Who told you about the loan?
	Loan repayment due	What is the amount due to the microfinance institution/bank?
	Consequences of loan default	Consequences when you default on your loan
	Financial situation	Has your financial situation improved?
	Utility for the intended purpose	What is the amount you invest in the activity for which you have taken a loan?

(*continued*)

Section	Constructs	Measurement items
Section C: Borrower behaviour attributes	Improved household financial position (borrower perception of microfinance)	Has your financial position in the household improved after taking a loan from the current institution?
		Have you been able to provide better educational facilities to your children after taking a loan from the current institution?
		Have you and your family experienced better health services after taking a loan from the current institution?
	Disclosure	Does the institution disclose all the terms and conditions and the purpose of the loan in group meetings to you?
		Are the institutions transparent in their communication with the borrowers?
		Does the loan card given to each borrower carry all the important information, such as interest rate, processing fees, etc?
	Spending on the unintended purpose of the loan	The purposes for which you spent the loan are: fairs and festivals customary activities—births; deaths; marriages in the family; and other faiths, beliefs, and practices other social commitments—gifts, attending funerals and marriages of others, inviting son-in-law to the house, etc. religious purposes—going on a pilgrimage, donations to religious functions, offers to deities, etc.
	Improved status of women in the household	Do you have a greater say in managing household finances after taking a loan from the current institution?
		Has the need to spare a certain amount for each instalment made the men more responsible towards their business?
		Are you able to question your spouse about his business and track their cash flows?
	Loan products	Are you satisfied with the amount of the loan drawn from the institution?
		Are you satisfied with the tenure of the loan drawn from the institution?
		Are you satisfied with the rate of interest charged on all loan products?
		Are you satisfied with the loan repayment frequency offered by the institution?

Section	Constructs	Measurement items
	Opportunity to socialize	Has the institution, through its group meetings, given you the opportunity to meet new women members?
		Are you friends with your group members?
		Do you help resolve problems faced by your group members in your locality?
	Privacy of borrower information	Are you comfortable sharing your private information with the institution?
		Are the documents provided by you kept in safe custody and not misused by the institution?
		Are the documents returned to you in case of rejection of the loan application?

Source: Prepared by the author.

ANNEXURE V

Study of the Andhra Pradesh Crisis

A decade post-crisis, a study was collaboratively undertaken by Clinical Research Institute of Fetal Medicine (CRFIM) and Leveraging Evidence for Access and Development (LEAD) at Krea University (formerly IFMR LEAD (IFMR, Institute for Financial Management and Research)). The research encompassed 347 women members of self-help groups in Andhra Pradesh and Telangana. The study examined (i) the diagnosis of the reasons for the substantial debt bubble in Andhra Pradesh, (ii) the effects of the rural credit market subsequent to the microfinance institution (MFI) crisis, (iii) the expansion of self-help group (SHG) credit linkage and microfinance in Andhra Pradesh, and (iv) exemplary practices in MFIs following the MFI crisis.

Major findings of the study were as follows:

a) Following the crisis, SHGs have become the predominant source of borrowing, with 91% of respondents indicating they have exclusively borrowed from SHGs.
b) In the absence of MFIs, SHG loans from state-run MFIs (SRMFIs) and banks were the alternative sources of credit among the sample SHG borrowers.
c) The proliferation of SHGs below the poverty line (BLP) in both states has led to a decline in the growth of savings-linked SHGs. The growth of outstanding savings in the states rose significantly to 31.60%, above the national average of 13.10%, reflecting the public's trust in the SHG ecosystem following the MFI crisis.

Microcredit outstanding (31 March 2022)

Public-sector banks

Sr. no.	Name of bank	Total bank loans outstanding against SHGs		Out of total—exclusive women		Out of total National Rural Livelihood Mission (NRLM)/Swarna Jayanti Gram Swarozgar Yojna (SGSY) SHGs		Out of total SHGs—under National Urban Livelihood Mission (NULM)/Swarna Jayanti Shahari Rojgar Yojana (SJSRY)	
		No. of SHGs	Loans O/S	No. of SHGs	Loans O/S	No. of SHGs	Loans O/S	No. of SHGs	Loans O/S
	Telangana								
1	Bank of Baroda	6,794	42,984.28	6,518	42,390.51	6,486	42,317.74	129	391.63
2	Bank of India	243	1,463.00	207	1,253.00	243	1,463.00	0	0.00
3	Bank of Maharashtra	942	1,864.95	573	1,111.47	778	1,667.28	24	31.79
4	Canara Bank	29,072	151,468.06	28,200	148,438.70	29,072	151,468.06	0	0.00
5	Central Bank of India	0	0	0	0	0	0	0	0
6	Indian Bank	15,711	81,091.73	15,581	80,674.15	15,606	80,520.87	105	570.86
7	Indian Overseas Bank	8,729	15,787.16	8,258	15,403.20	4,840	12,124.93	182	667.88
8	Punjab National Bank	2,196	7,644.67	2,196	7,644.67	1,880	6,841.86	316	802.81
9	State Bank of India	128,985	608,136.00	125,144	590,030.00	108,597	506,890.00	3,533	14,080.00
10	UCO Bank	1,411	6,176.08	13	0.00	1,385	6,176.08	10	0.00
11	Union Bank of India	86,665	450,412.49	82,503	433,580.33	68,921	376,555.05	13,582	57,025.28
	Total	280,748	1,367,028.42	269,193	1,320,526.03	237,808	1,186,024.87	17,881	73,570.25
	Total southern region	**1,946,110**	**8,669,607.06**	**1,840,688**	**8,326,773.63**	**1,467,480**	**7,060,593.99**	**84,851**	**463,889.97**

Source: Prepared by the author.

Private-sector banks engaged in microcredit (not all the private-sector banks are engaged)

	Telangana								
1	HDFC Bank Ltd.	11,805	46,992.45	11,805	46,992.45	2,739	11,038.79	9,006	35,895.52
2	ICICI Bank Limited	1	0.00	1	0.00	1	0.00	0	0.00
3	IDBI Bank Limited	1	0.27	1	0.27	0	0.00	0	0.00
4	Karnataka Bank Ltd								
5	Karur Vysya Bank Ltd								
6	South Indian Bank Ltd								
7	The Dhanalakshmi Bank Ltd	3	0.00	3	0.00	0	0.00	0	0.00
	Total	**11,810**	**46,992.72**	**11,810**	**46,992.72**	**2,740**	**11,038.79**	**9,006**	**35,895.52**

Source: Prepared by the author.

	Telangana								
1	The Adilabad District Co-operative Central Bank Ltd	402	633.42	402	633.42	402	633.42	0	0.00
2	The District Co-Operative Central Bank Ltd, Khammam	633	1,500.08	633	1,500.08	633	1,500.08	0	0.00
3	The District Co-Operative Central Bank Ltd, Medak								
4	The District Co-Operative Central Bank Ltd, Warangal	1,464	7,865.54	1,464	7,865.54	1,464	7,865.54	0	0.00
5	The Hyderabad District Co-Operative Central Bank Ltd	26	16.98	26	16.98	25	16.97	1	0.01
6	The Karimnagar District Co-Operative Central Bank Ltd	4,341	23,086.78	4,341	23,086.78	0	0.00	0	0.00
7	The Mahbubnagar District Co-Operative Central Bank Ltd	12	7.36	12	7.36	12	7.36	0	0.00
8	The Nalgonda District Co-Operative Central Bank Ltd	304	421.16	304	421.16	0	0.00	0	0.00
9	The Nizamabad District Co-Operative Central Bank Ltd	2,852	8,146.34	2,852	8,146.34	0	0.00	0	0.00
10	The Telangana State Co-Operative Bank Ltd	2,792	6,812.28	2,771	6,791.19	0	0.00	2,792	6,812.28
	Total	**12,826**	**48,489.94**	**12,805**	**48,468.85**	**2,536**	**10,023.37**	**2,793**	**6,812.29**

Source: Prepared by the author.

Regional rural banks

S. no.	Name of bank	Total loans disbursed during the year		Out of total—loan disbursed to exclusive women SHGs		Out of total—loan disbursed under NRLM/SGSY		Out of total SHGs—under NULM/SJSRY	
		No. of SHGs	Loans disbursed	No. of SHGs	Loans disbursed	No. of SHGs	Loans disbursed	No. of SHGs	Loans disbursed
1	Andhra Pradesh Grameen Vikas Bank	86,371	501,593.18	86,371	501,593.18	56,538	318,010.41	13,970	81,885.94
2	Telangana Grameena Bank	30,545	221,733.40	30,545	221,733.40	24,334	182,875.09	6,211	38,858.31
	Total	116,916	723,326.58	116,916	723,326.58	80,872	500,885.50	20,181	120,744.25
	Total southern region	**355,894**	**2,203,128.18**	**346,831**	**2,191,921.77**	**291,381**	**1,781,968.53**	**30,486**	**196,915.11**

Source: Compiled by the author with the data from various NABARD reports.

Private-sector non-banking financial institutions

S. no	Name of the MFI	No. of borrowers (₹ in lakhs)	Total credit net (₹ in crores)	Gross credit (₹ in crores)
1	Asirvad Microfinance Ltd	25.74	5,755.69	7,002.18
2	Share Microfin Ltd	3.06	577.07	577.07
3	Spandana Sphoorty Financial Ltd	23.50	5,709.02	6,198.87
4	Vaya Finserve Pvt. Ltd	4.90	1,195.11	1,201.68
5	Arohan Financial Services Ltd	18.64	3,710.19	3,740.15
	Total private MFIs	**75.84**	**16,947.08**	**18,719.95**

Source: Compiled by the author from various sources.

ANNEXURE VI

Questionnaire Administered to the Borrowers

S. no.	Questions and the information sought	Replies and consolidations
1	Name	
2	Gender	Female 32, male 18
3	Village name/area in Hyderabad	
4	Age	Mean age 40, median age 39, std deviation: 8.27539
5	Marital status	Married
6	Number of children	Mean 1.9, median 2
7	School-going	Mean 1.1.2, median 1
8	Infants	0
9	School discontinued	0
10	Married daughters	14/50
11	Married sons	12/50
12	Marriageable daughter	5/50
13	Educational level	F:- Ille 1, P 9, S 21, UG 1, P 5, S 13
14	Dependants	Mean 2.65, median 3
15	House	No 21/50, yes 25/50
16	Agr. land	No
17	House plot	12/50
18	Rented house	Yes 25/50, no 25
19	Occupation	25
20	Agriculture	0
21	Allied agriculture activity	0
22	Small business	35
23	Caste activity	7
24	Service	8
25	Earning members in the family	Mean 1.533, median 2
26	Money required to run family	Mean: ₹140,800; median: ₹130,000; mode: ₹120,000; std: ₹31,858.744

(*continued*)

S. no.	Questions and the information sought	Replies and consolidations	
27	Total household income	Mean: ₹102,240; median: ₹100,000; mode: ₹100,000; std: ₹13,033.0193	
28	Microcredit taken amount	Mean: ₹11,100; median: ₹10,000; mode: ₹10,000; std: ₹3,682.557	
29	Microcredit due to be repaid to bank	Mean: ₹6,400; median: ₹5,500; mode: ₹5,000; std: ₹4,150.23973	
30	Microcredit utilized for business	Mean: ₹5,150; median: ₹5,000; mode: ₹10,000; std: ₹4,143.16501	
31	Utilized for agriculture	0	
32	Food	6.05%	18,000
33	Clothing	1%	2,000
34	Health	6.72%	20,000
35	Marriage of children	12.77%	38,000
36.	Education	4.54%	13,500
37	Death	3.70%	11,000
38	Social commitments	28.74%	85,500
39	Gifts	2.86%	8,500
40	Religious ceremonies	16.47%	49,000
41	Festivals	13.78%	41,000
42	Pilgrimages	3.36%	10,000
43	Paying local debts	0.34%	1,000
44	Lending to others	0	
45	Personal consumption—pan, beedi, cigarettes, alcohol	0	
46	**Total spending on social events**	**₹297,500: this forms 53.60% of total loan of ₹555,000**	
47	Have you taken any consumption loan?	0	
48	Have you taken any loan from other sources than MFI?	Yes 14, no 36	
49	Is the loan given by the bank adequate for your business?	No	

Source: Prepared by the author.

Bibliography

Abbink, K., Irlenbusch, B., and Renner, E. (2002) 'The Performance of Self-Help Groups in South India', *Economic Inquiry*, 44 (4): 614–28.

Ahlin, C. and Townsend, R. M. (2007) 'Using Repayment Data to Test across Models of Joint Liability Lending', *The Economic Journal*, 117 (517): F11–F51.

Akula, V. (2010) *A Fistful of Rice: My Unexpected Quest to End Poverty through Profitability* (New York: PublicAffairs).

Armendáriz de Aghion, B. (1999) 'On the Design of a Credit Agreement with Peer Monitoring', *Journal of Development Economics*, 60 (1): 79–104.

Armendáriz de Aghion, B. and Gollier, C. (2000) 'Peer Group Formation in an Adverse Selection Model', *The Economic Journal*, 110 (465): 632–43.

Armendáriz de Aghion, B. and Morduch, J. (2000) 'Microfinance: Beyond Group Lending', *The Economics of Transition*, 8 (2): 401–20.

Armendáriz de Aghion, B. and Morduch, J. (2005) *The Economics of Microfinance* (Cambridge, MA: MIT Press).

Asim, S. (2008) 'Evaluating the Impact of Microfinance on Women's Empowerment: Evidence from Pakistan', working paper (Washington, DC: World Bank).

Badatya, K. C. (2006) 'Self Help Groups in Andhra Pradesh: A Case Study', report for the National Bank for Agriculture and Rural Development (NABARD).

Banerjee, A. V. (1999) 'Prospects and Strategies for Land Reforms', in B. Pleskovic and J. E. Stiglitz (eds), *Annual World Bank Conference on Development Economics 1999* (Washington, DC: World Bank), 253–74.

Banerjee, A. V., Besley, T., and Guinnane, T. W. (1994) 'Thy Neighbor's Keeper: The Design of a Credit Cooperative with a Theory and a Test', *Quarterly Journal of Economics*, 109 (2): 491–515.

Banerjee, A. V. and Duflo, E. (2007) 'The Economic Lives of the Poor', *Journal of Economic Perspectives*, 21 (1): 141–68.

Banerjee, A. V. and Duflo, E. (2011) *Poor Economics: A Radical Rethinking of the Way to Fight Global Poverty* (New York: PublicAffairs).

Banerjee, A. V., Duflo, E., Glennerster, R., and Kinnan, C. (2015) 'The Miracle of Microfinance? Evidence from a Randomized Evaluation', *American Economic Journal: Applied Economics*, 7 (1): 22–53.

Banerjee, A. V. et al. (2010) 'Help Microfinance, Don't Kill It', *Indian Express*, 26 November.

Barnes, C., Gaile, G., and Kimbombo, R. (2001) 'The Impact of Microfinance on the Household and Individual in Uganda', United States Agency for International Development (USAID)–Assessing the Impact of Microfinance (AIMS) paper.

Bateman, M. and Chang, H.-J. (2012) 'Microfinance and the Illusion of Development: From Hubris to Nemesis in Thirty Years', *World Economic Review*, 1: 13–36.

Belay, E. I. (2002) 'Factors Affecting Financial Performance of Microfinance Institutions in Ethiopia', MSc thesis, Addis Ababa University.

Besley, T. and Coate, S. (1995) 'Group Lending, Repayment Incentives and Social Collateral', *Journal of Development Economics*, 46 (1): 1–18.

Bhimani, A. (2021) *Financial Management for Technology Start-Ups: A Handbook for Growth* (Oxford: Oxford University Press).

Biswas, B. (2010) 'Client Protection Mechanism in Indian Microfinance Institutions: A Study on Arohan', *Business Spectrum*, 35–36: 38–47.

Biswas, B. (2014) *Inclusive Finance India Report 2014* (New Delhi: Oxford University Press).

Bittman, M. (2002). 'Social Participation and Family Welfare: The Case of Households' Expenditure on Leisure', SPRC discussion paper no. 122. Sydney: Social Policy Research Centre, University of New South Wales.

Borchgrevink, A., Woldehanna, T., Gebrehiwot, A., and Cassimon, D. (2005) 'Marginalized Groups, Credit and Empowerment: The Case of Dedebit Credit and Savings Institution (DECSI) of Tigray, Ethiopia', Norwegian Institute of International Affairs (NUPI) report.

Brown, M., Guin, B., and Morkoetter, S. (2011) 'Microfinance Institutions and Efficiency', working paper (St. Gallen: University of St. Gallen).

Brown, P. H., Bulte, E., and Zhang, X. (2007). 'Positional Spending and Status Seeking in Rural China', discussion paper no. 00710.

Bruton, Garry D., Khavul, S., and Chavez, H. (2011) 'Microlending in Emerging Economies: Building a New Line of Inquiry from the Ground Up', *Journal of International Business Studies*, 42 (5): 718–39.

Capoor, J. (2001) 'Report of the Committee on Net Worth Norms for Co-operative Banks' (Mumbai: Reserve Bank of India).

Carter, M. R. (1995) 'Intellectual Strategies for Agricultural Development: Observations from Cuba, Chile and Nicaragua', *Agricultural Economics*, 12 (1): 75–80.

Chandani, A. (2014) 'Impact of Microfinance on Women Empowerment: A Study with Reference to Chennai City', *International Journal of Management and Social Science Research*, 3 (6).

Charitonenko, S. and Rahman, S. M. (2002) *Commercialization of Microfinance: Bangladesh* (Manila: Asian Development Bank).

Chen, X. (2011) 'Social Distance, Status Affirmation, and Gift Expenditures in Rural China', *China Economic Review*, 22 (3): 402–13.

Chen, J. and Zhang, J. (2012) 'The Impact of Microfinance on the Welfare of Poor Households: Evidence from Rural China', *Journal of International Development*, 24 (S1): S154–S172.

Chowdhury, M. J. A., Ghosh, D., and Wright, R. E. (2005) 'The Impact of Micro-Credit on Poverty: Evidence from Bangladesh', *Progress in Development Studies*, 5 (4): 298–309.

Das, S. K. (2011) 'Microfinance and Women Empowerment: A Study on SHGs in West Bengal', *International Journal of Multidisciplinary Management Studies*, 1 (3): 1–15.

Das, S. K., and Jena, S. K. (2011) *Microfinance and Empowerment of Rural Poor in India* (New Delhi: New Century Publications).

Dekker, M. and Hoogeveen, H. (2002) 'Bridging the Gap: Microfinance and Social Safety Nets', *Journal of International Development*, 14 (6): 769–86.

Desai, J. and Tarozzi, A. (2013) 'Microcredit, Family Planning and Low Fertility: Evidence from Ethiopia', *Demography*, 50 (5): 1649–79.

Desai, V. and Tarozzi, A. (2013) 'Microfinance, Interest Rates and Over-Indebtedness', *Journal of Economic Behavior & Organization*, 92: 243–58.

Dichter, T. W. (1996) 'Questioning the Future of NGOs in Microfinance', *Journal of International Development*, 8 (2): 259–69.

Dixon, R., Ritchie, J., and Siwale, J. (2006) 'Microfinance: Lessons from Zambia', *Journal of International Development*, 18 (7): 1031–47.

Dohn, A. L., Chavez, A., Dohn, M. N., Satinsky, W., and Prows, K. (2004). 'Changes in Health Indicators Related to Health Promotion and Microcredit Programs in the Dominican Republic,' *Revista Panamericana de Salud Pública* (Pan American Journal of Public Health), 15 (3): 185–93.

Dohn, T. (2004) 'Microfinance in Ethiopia: Review of the Institutional and Regulatory Framework' (Addis Ababa: Association of Ethiopian Microfinance Institutions (AEMFI)).

Dunford, C. (2001) 'Building Better Lives: Sustainable Integration of Microfinance and Education in Child Survival, Reproductive Health and HIV/AIDS Prevention for the Poorest Families', discussion paper, Washington, DC: Microcredit Summit Campaign.

Economic Times (2023) 'Microfinance Industry Records 22% Growth', *Economic Times*, 15 June.

Finch, G., Kocieniewski, D., Natarajan, S., and Hoffman, C. (2022) 'Big Money Backs Tiny Loans That Lead to Debt, Despair and Even Suicide', *Bloomberg*, 3 May.

Gabrielian, V. (1999) 'Transition to Microfinance: The Armenian Experience', *Development in Practice*, 9 (1–2): 173–77.

Gadekar, R. (2020) 'Impact of Microfinance on Poverty Alleviation: A Study of Maharashtra', *Journal of Critical Reviews*, 7 (11): 635–40.

Gangopadhyay, S., Ghatak, M., and Lensink, R. (2005) 'Joint Liability Lending and the Peer Selection Effect', *Economic Journal*, 115 (506): 1005–15.

Gargi Rao, P. (2015) 'The Menace of Microfinance in India', *The Hans India*, 17 September.

Gertler, P., Levine, D. I., and Moretti, E. (2009) 'Do Microfinance Programs Help Families Insure Consumption against Illness?', *Journal of the European Economic Association*, 7 (6): 1255–73.

Getaneh, G. (2002) 'The Regulation of Microfinance in Ethiopia: A Comparative Analysis', MSc thesis, University of Birmingham.

Ghatak, M. (1999) 'Group Lending, Local Information and Peer Selection', *Journal of Development Economics*, 60 (1): 27–50.

Ghatak, M. (2000) 'Screening by the Company You Keep: Joint Liability Lending and the Peer Selection Effect', *The Economic Journal*, 110 (465): 601–31.

Ghiyazuddin, M. and Sen Gupta, R. (2012) 'Microfinance Crisis in Andhra Pradesh: A Case Study', *Journal of Financial Studies*, 4 (2): 12–28.

Goetz, A. M. and Sen Gupta, R. (1996) 'Who Takes the Credit? Gender, Power, and Control Over Loan-Use in Rural Credit Programs in Bangladesh', *World Development*, 24 (1): 45–63.

GoI (Government of India) (1999) 'Report of the Working Group on the Role of Credit in the Ninth Five Year Plan' (New Delhi: Ministry of Rural Development).

Halan, M., Sane, R., and Thomas, S. (2011) 'The Microfinance Industry in India: Remarkable Results in a Short Time' (New Delhi: Sage Publications) (referred to in text as Renuka and Susan).

Halkos, G. E. and Salamouris, D. S. (2004) 'Efficiency Measurement of the Greek Commercial Banks with the Use of Data Envelopment Analysis', *Applied Financial Economics*, 14 (4): 249–59.

Härmä, J. (2009) 'School Choice in Rural Nigeria', *Comparative Education*, 45 (2): 203–20.

Harper, M. (2005) 'Farm Credit and Microfinance—Is There a Conflict?', *Small Enterprise Development*, 16 (3): 10–14.

Holvoet, N. (2004) 'Impact of Microfinance Programs on Children's Education: Do the Particular Channels of Credit Matter?', *Journal of Microfinance*, 6 (2): 27–51.

Hubert Tchuigoua, H. (2014) 'Institutional Framework and Performance of Microfinance Institutions in Africa', *Strategic Change*, 23 (1–2): 47–62.

Investopedia. 2024. 'Microfinance: Definition, Benefits, and Example'. https://www.investopedia.com/terms/m/microfinance.asp last modified 26 February 2024.

Jayaraman, R. (2001) 'Intergenerational Transmission of Poverty in Industrialized Nations', working paper (Ithaca, NY: Cornell University).

Johnson, S. and Rogaly, B. (1997) *Microfinance and Poverty Reduction* (Oxford: Oxfam GB).

Karl, M. (1995) *Women and Empowerment: Participation and Decision Making* (London: Zed Books).

Kellett, J. (2011) 'The Sustainability of Microfinance Institutions', *Journal of International Development*, 23 (4): 501–15.

Khandker, S. R. (2001) 'Does Micro-Finance Really Benefit the Poor? Evidence from Bangladesh' (Washington, DC: World Bank Publications).

Kharti, R. (2014) 'Impact of Microfinance on Rural Households: A Case Study', *International Journal of Social Sciences*, 3 (2): 45–58.

Khaval, S. (2010) 'Microfinance and Women's Empowerment: Evidence from India', *Journal of Development Studies*, 12 (1): 102–18.

Kibria, N. (1998) 'Becoming a Garments Worker: The Mobilization of Women into the Garments Factories of Bangladesh', United Nations Research Institute for Social Development (UNRISD) Occasional Paper No. 9 (Geneva: UNRISD).

Kothari, C. R. (2004) *Research Methodology: Methods and Techniques*, 2nd edn (New Delhi: New Age International Publishers).

Kothari, C. R. and Garg, G. (2014) *Research Methodology: Methods and Techniques*, 3rd edn (New Delhi: New Age International Publishers).

Kumbirai, M. and Webb, R. (2010) 'A Financial Ratio Analysis of Commercial Bank Performance in South Africa', *African Review of Economics and Finance*, 2 (1): 30–53.

Kurukshetra (2022) 'Rural Development and the NABARD Self-Help Group-Bank Linkage Programme', November 2022, Government of India.

La Torre, M. and Vento, G. A. (2006) *Microfinance* (Basingstoke: Palgrave Macmillan).

Labie, M., Méon, P. G., Mersland, R., and Loduar, R. (2010) 'Discrimination by Microcredit Officers: Theory and Evidence on Disability in Uganda', *The Journal of Development Studies*, 46 (8): 1470–92.

Leatherman, S. and Dunford, C. (2010) 'Linking Health Education and Microfinance: The Impact on Health Behaviors and Health Outcomes', *Journal of Health Care for the Poor and Underserved*, 21 (4): 1120–41.

Leatherman, S., Metcalfe, M., Geissler, K., Dunford, C., and Gray, B. (2011). 'Integrating Microfinance and Health Strategies: Examining the Evidence to Inform Policy and Practice,' *Health Policy and Planning* 27 (2): 85–101.

Ledgerwood, J. (1999) *Microfinance Handbook: An Institutional and Financial Perspective* (Washington, DC: World Bank).

Littlefield, E., Morduch, J., and Hashemi, S. (2003) 'Is Microfinance an Effective Strategy to Reach the Millennium Development Goals?', *Consultative Group to Assist the Poor (CGAP) Focus Note*, 24: 1–11.

Madajewicz, M. (2003a) 'Capital for the Poor: The Effect of Wealth on the Optimal Credit Contract', working paper (New York: Columbia University).

Madajewicz, M. (2003b) 'Joint Liability versus Individual Liability: Why Do the Poor Choose Groups?', working paper (New York: Columbia University).

Mahanta, P., Panda, G., and Sahoo, E. (2012) 'Status of Microfinance in India: A Review', *International Journal of Marketing, Financial Services & Management Research*, 1 (11): 230–37.

Malleswari, B. (2010) 'Role of Microfinance in Promoting Women Entrepreneurship', *Journal of Business Management*, 2 (1–2): 171–8.

Mango, S. J., Cheng, E., and Ahmed, A. (2009) 'The Role of Microfinance in Rural Development', *International Journal of Economics and Finance*, 1 (2): 115–24.

Mayoux, L. (1999) 'Questioning Virtuous Spirals: Micro-Finance and Women's Empowerment in Africa', *Journal of International Development*, 11 (7): 957–84.

Mayoux, L. (2009) 'Questioning Virtuous Spirals: Microfinance and Women's Empowerment', in G. S. Cheema and V. Popovski (eds), *Building Trust in Government: Innovations in Governance Reform in Asia* (Tokyo: United Nations University Press), 145–69.

Metcalfe, J. (2012) 'Efficiency and Sustainability in Microfinance', *World Development*, 40 (3): 489–502.

Michael, K. (2006) 'The Role of Microfinance in Poverty Alleviation', *Journal of Economic Perspectives*, 14 (2): 65–82.

Montgomery, R. (1996) 'Disciplining or Democratizing? Bangladesh's Grameen Bank and BRAC', *Development in Practice*, 6 (3): 210–19.

Morduch, J. (1999) 'The Microfinance Promise', *Journal of Economic Literature*, 37 (4): 1569–614.

Morduch, J. (2000) 'The Microfinance Schism', *World Development*, 28 (4): 617–29.

Murthy, R. K., Raju, K. V., and Kamath, A. (2005) 'Towards Women's Empowerment and Poverty Reduction: Lessons from the Andhra Pradesh South India', working paper (Bangalore: The Institute for Social and Economic Change).

Musona, D. (2004) 'Institutional Sustainability of Microfinance in Africa', PhD thesis, University of Pretoria.

Musona, D. and Coetzee, G. (2001) 'The Impact of Microfinance on Household Welfare', *Journal of Financial Management*, 9 (2): 33–48.

Musona, D. (2004) 'The Limits of Micro-Credit: A Case Study of Local-Level Institutions in Zambia', in G. Mwabu, J. G. Ng'ethe, and R. Kiriti (eds), *Health, Savings and Economic Development in Africa: Selected Studies* (Nairobi: University of Nairobi Press), 89–108.

NABARD (National Bank for Agriculture and Rural Development) (1995) *Report of the Working Group on NGOs and SHGs* (Mumbai: NABARD).

NABARD (1999) *Task Force on Supportive Policy and Regulatory Framework for Microfinance* (Mumbai: NABARD).

NABARD (2006) *Status of Microfinance in India 2005–06* (Mumbai: NABARD).

NABARD (2022–23) *Annual Report 2022–23* (Mumbai: NABARD).

Narwal, K. P., Pathneja, S., and Yadav, M. K. (2015) 'Performance Evaluation of MFIs in India', *International Journal of Business and Management*, 10 (6): 185–96.

Onyuma, S. O., and Shem, A. O. (2005) 'Myths of Informal Financial Segments in Africa: A Case Study of Ethiopia and Kenya', *Journal of African Economies*, 14 (1): 120–56.

Panda, R. K. (2009) 'Microfinance and Women Empowerment: A Study in Orissa, Jharkhand and Chhattisgarh', *Journal of Social and Economic Development* 11 (2): 186–203.

Paxton, J., and Fruman, C. (1997) 'Outreach and Sustainability: A Comparative Analysis of Savings-First and Credit-First Mechanisms', *Sustainable Banking with the Poor Case Study Series* (Washington, DC: World Bank).

Pearlman, S. (2012) 'Too Vulnerable for Microfinance? Risk and Vulnerability as Determinants of Microfinance Selection in Lima', *Journal of Development Studies*, 48 (9): 1342.

Pitt, M. M. and Khandker, S. R. (2003) 'The Impact of Group-Based Credit Programs on Poor Households in Bangladesh: Does the Gender of Participants Matter?', *Journal of Political Economy*, 106 (5): 958–96.

Pronyk, P. M. et al. (2006) 'Effect of a Structural Intervention for the Prevention of Intimate-Partner Violence and HIV in South Africa: A Cluster Randomised Trial', *The Lancet*, 368 (9551): 1973–83.

Purbaningsih, Y. P. and Fatimah, S. (2014) 'Efficiency of Microfinance Institutions in Indonesia', *Journal of Indonesian Economy and Business*, 29 (3): 215–30.

Rahman, A., and Khan, S. R. (2007) 'Micro-Determinants of Profitability of Microfinance Institutions in Bangladesh', *Applied Economics*, 39 (10): 1301–09.

Rao, V. (1993) 'The Pricing of Marriages in South India', *Journal of Political Economy*, 101 (4): 666–80.

Rao, V. (2001) 'Poverty and Public Celebrations in Rural India', Policy Research Working Paper No. 2528 (Washington, DC: World Bank).

Rao, V., and Woolcock, M. (2013) 'History, Humility and Hairballs: Explaining the Culture of Development', in V. Rao and M. Walton (eds), *Culture and Public Action* (Stanford: Stanford University Press), 1–32.

Rathore, R. (2017) 'Growth and Performance of Self Help Groups in Haryana: A Comparative Study', *International Journal of Research in Management & Business Studies*, 4 (3): 45–52.

RBI (Reserve Bank of India) (1996) 'Report of the Working Group on Microfinance', Mumbai: RBI.

RBI (2012) *Master Circular on Maintenance of Statutory Reserves*, RBI/2012-13/64 UBD.BPD.(PCB).MC.No.12/09.14.000/2012-13 (Mumbai: RBI).

RMK (Rashtriya Mahila Kosh) (2000) *Annual Report 1999–2000* (New Delhi: RMK).

Rozas, D. and Sinha, S. (2010) 'Microfinance Indian Crisis: A Report on the Andhra Pradesh Situation', Micro-Credit Ratings International Ltd (M-CRIL).

Ruziqa, A. (2013) 'The Impact of Credit and Liquidity Risk on Bank Profitability', in *Proceedings of 10th International Business Research Conference* (Dubai: World Business Institute), 1–13.

Sanderatine, N. (1983) 'Institutionalizing Microfinance: The Sri Lankan Experience', *Central Bank of Ceylon Review*, 15: 12–28.

Sane, R. and Thomas, S. (2011) 'A Policy Response to the Indian Micro-Finance Crisis', Working Paper No. 2011-25 (Mumbai: Indira Gandhi Institute of Development Research).

Sanyal, P. (2009) 'From Credit to Collective Action: The Role of Microfinance in Promoting Women's Social Capital and Normative Influence', *American Sociological Review*, 74 (4): 529–50.

Saxena, S. (2014) 'The 2010 Microfinance Crisis in Andhra Pradesh, India and Its Implications for Microfinance in India', *Reconsidering Development*, 3 (1).

SEWA (Self-Employed Women's Association) (1999) *Self Employed Women's Association Annual Report* (Ahmedabad: SEWA).

SEWA Bank and Khandker, S. R. (2001) 'Impact of Self-Employed Women's Association (SEWA) Bank on Poverty', working paper (Washington, DC: World Bank).

Sharma, A. (2019) 'Microfinance and the Vulnerability of Urban Poor: A Study of SHG Loan Diversion in the Slums of Delhi', *Journal of Social and Economic Development*, 21 (2): 245–62.

Sharma, M. and Zeller, M. (1997) 'Repayment Performance in Group-Based Credit Programs in Bangladesh: An Empirical Analysis', *World Development*, 25 (10): 1731–42.

Smith, S. C. (2002) 'Village Banking and Maternal and Child Health: Evidence from Ecuador and Honduras', *World Development*, 30 (4): 707–23.

Sooryamoorthy, R. (2005) 'Microfinance and Women's Groups in Kerala', *International Journal of Voluntary and Non-Profit Organizations* 16 (1): 75–99.

Stiglitz, J. E. (1990) 'Peer Monitoring and Credit Markets', *World Bank Economic Review*, 4 (3): 351–66.

Stiglitz, J. E. and Weiss, A. (1981) 'Credit Rationing in Markets with Imperfect Information', *American Economic Review*, 71 (3): 393–410.

Swain, R. B. (2006) 'Coping with Economic Shocks: The Role of Self-Help Groups in Maharashtra, India', working paper (Uppsala: Uppsala University).

Swapna, S. (2017) 'Role of Microfinance in Women Entrepreneurship: A Study', *International Journal of Management* 8 (3): 116–22.

Tamrat, B. (2016) 'The Performance of Microfinance Institutions in Ethiopia', *International Journal of Research in Commerce, IT & Management*, 6 (2): 55–62.

The Economist (2007) 'Microfinance: The Battle of Juan de Dios', *The Economist*, 15 March.

Todd, H. and Ralph, K. (2007) 'The Grameen Bank at 30', *Journal of Microfinance*, 9 (1): 1–12.

Vachya, L., and Kamaiah, B. (2015) 'Microfinance Impact on Socio-Economic Empowerment: A Special Reference to Andhra Pradesh', *International Journal of Finance & Banking Studies*, 4 (1): 27–41.

Varghese, G. (2020) 'Efficiency and Sustainability of Microfinance Institutions: Evidence from India', *IIM Kozhikode Society & Management Review*, 9 (1): 102–14.

Varian, H. R. (1990) 'Monitoring Agents with Other Agents', *Journal of Institutional and Theoretical Economics*, 146 (1): 153–74.

Vodova, P. (2011) 'Liquidity of Commercial Banks in the Czech Republic', in *Proceedings of the 8th International Conference on Efficiency and Responsibility in Education* (Prague: Czech University of Life Sciences), 195–203.

Werner, C. (1997) 'Marriage, Markets, and Merchants: Changes in Wedding Feasts and Household Consumption Patterns in Rural Kazakstan', *Culture & Agriculture*, 19 (1–2): 6–13.

Werner, K., Sierra, S., and Nelson, J. (2007) *Social Capital and Poverty Reduction: Which Networks Matter?* (Washington, DC: World Bank).

Wiig, A. (1997a) *Credit Flowing from the Poor to the Rich: The Financial Market and the Role of the Grameen Bank in Rural Bangladesh*, Working Paper No. 1997:10 (Bergen: Chr. Michelsen Institute).

Wiig, A. (1997b) *Credit programmes: Methods for solving dilemmas of credit expansion* (Bergen: Chr. Michelsen Institute).

Wolcott, S. (2013) 'Rural Credit in Colonial India', in B. Armendáriz and M. Labie (eds), *The Handbook of Microfinance* (Singapore: World Scientific Publishing), 439–56.

WWB (Women's World Banking) (2003) 'Microfinance Performance Standards', WWB Publication Series, New York.

World Bank and Badatya, K. C. (2006) 'Microfinance and Rural Development in India', World Bank Policy Research Working Paper (Washington, DC: World Bank).

Wydick, B. (1999) 'Can Social Cohesion Be Harnessed to Repair Market Failures? Evidence from Group Lending in Guatemala', *The Economic Journal*, 109 (457): 463–75.

Yeh, H. (1996) 'The Financial Efficiency of Microfinance Institutions', *Journal of Development Economics*, 12 (1): 88–101.

Yunus, M. (1975) *The Grameen Bank Project* (Dhaka: Grameen Bank).

Yunus, M. (1999) *Banker to the Poor: Micro-Lending and the Battle against World Poverty* (New York: PublicAffairs).

Yunus, M. (2003) *Halving Poverty by 2015—We Can Do It!* (Dhaka: Grameen Bank).

Index

For the benefit of digital users, indexed terms that span two pages (e.g., 52–53) may, on occasion, appear on only one of those pages.

W

Y

Z

The manufacturer's authorised representative in the EU for product safety is Oxford University Press España S.A. of El Parque Empresarial San Fernando de Henares, Avenida de Castilla, 2 - 28830 Madrid (www.oup.es/en or product.safety@oup.com). OUP España S.A. also acts as importer into Spain of products made by the manufacturer.
Printed and bound by CPI Group (UK) Ltd, Croydon, CR0 4YY
02/10/2026
02226626-0004